THE STATES AND THE NATION SERIES, of which this volume is a
part, is designed to assist the American people in a serious look at the ideals
they have espoused and the experiences they have undergone in the history of
the nation. The content of every volume represents the scholarship, experience,
and opinions of its author. The costs of writing and editing were met mainly
by grants from the National Endowment for the Humanities, a federal agency.
The project was administered by the American Association for State and Local
History, a nonprofit learned society, working with an Editorial Board of distinguished editors, authors, and historians, whose names are listed below.

Alabama

A Bicentennial History

Virginia Van der Veer Hamilton

W. W. Norton & Company, Inc.
New York

American Association for State and Local History
Nashville

Copyright © 1977
American Association for State and Local History
All rights reserved

Library of Congress Cataloguing-in-Publication Data

Hamilton, Virginia Van der Veer.
   Alabama.

   (The States and the Nation series)
   Bibliography: p.
   Includes index.
   1. Alabama—History.   I. Title.   II. Series.
F326.H26   976.1   76–54517
ISBN 0–393–05621–X

Published and distributed by W. W. Norton & Company, Inc.
500 Fifth Avenue
New York, New York 10036
Printed in the United States of America
1 2 3 4 5 6 7 8 9 0

For my Mother and in memory
of my Father

Contents

Illustrations

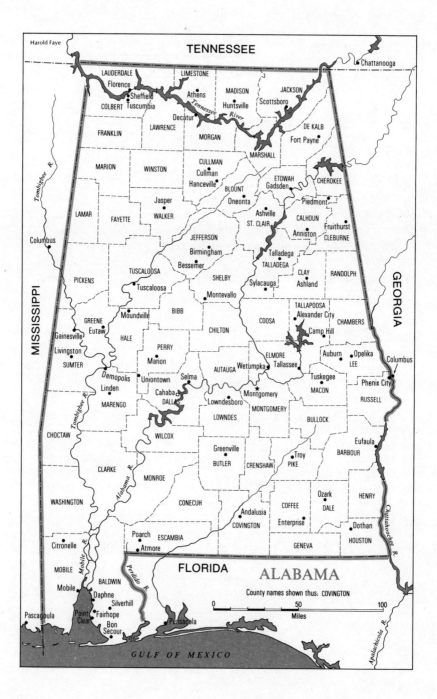

Harold Faye

TENNESSEE

Chattanooga

LAUDERDALE
LIMESTONE
Florence
MADISON
JACKSON
Athens
Scottsboro
Sheffield
Huntsville
COLBERT
Tuscumbia
Decatur
DE KALB
FRANKLIN
LAWRENCE
MORGAN
Fort Payne

MARSHALL

MARION
WINSTON
CULLMAN
ETOWAH
CHEROKEE
Cullman
Gadsden
Hanceville
BLOUNT
Piedmont
Jasper
Oneonta
Ashville
CALHOUN
WALKER
ST. CLAIR
Anniston
Fruithurst
LAMAR
FAYETTE
CLEBURNE
JEFFERSON
Birmingham
Talladega
CLAY
RANDOLPH
Bessemer
TALLADEGA
Columbus
SHELBY
Sylacauga
Ashland
PICKENS
TUSCALOOSA
Tuscaloosa
Montevallo
TALLAPOOSA
Alexander City
CHAMBERS
Moundville
BIBB
COOSA
Camp Hill
GREENE
Eutaw
CHILTON
Auburn
Opelika
Gainesville
HALE
LEE
Columbus
Livingston
PERRY
ELMORE
SUMTER
Marion
AUTAUGA
Wetumpka
Tallassee
Phenix City
Demopolis
Selma
Tuskegee
Linden
Uniontown
MACON
RUSSELL
Cahaba
Montgomery
MARENGO
DALLAS
Lowndesboro
MONTGOMERY
CHOCTAW
LOWNDES
BULLOCK
WILCOX
Eufaula
Greenville
BARBOUR
CLARKE
BUTLER
Troy
MONROE
CRENSHAW
PIKE
WASHINGTON
CONECUH
Ozark
HENRY
COFFEE
DALE
Andalusia
Citronelle
COVINGTON
Enterprise
Dothan
Poarch
ESCAMBIA
HOUSTON
Atmore
GENEVA
MOBILE
FLORIDA
ALABAMA
Mobile
BALDWIN
Daphne
County names shown thus: COVINGTON
Silverhill
Pascagoula
Point
Fairhope
Clear
Bon
Secour
Pensacola
0   50   100
Miles

GULF OF MEXICO

MISSISSIPPI

GEORGIA

Tombigbee R.

Tombigbee R.

Alabama R.

Mobile R.

Perdido R.

Chattahoochee R.

Apalachicola R.

Tennessee River

Invitation to the Reader

IN 1807, former President John Adams argued that a complete history of the American Revolution could not be written until the history of change in each state was known, because the principles of the Revolution were as various as the states that went through it. Two hundred years after the Declaration of Independence, the American nation has spread over a continent and beyond. The states have grown in number from thirteen to fifty. And democratic principles have been interpreted differently in every one of them.

We therefore invite you to consider that the history of your state may have more to do with the bicentennial review of the American Revolution than does the story of Bunker Hill or Valley Forge. The Revolution has continued as Americans extended liberty and democracy over a vast territory. John Adams was right: the states are part of that story, and the story is incomplete without an account of their diversity.

The Declaration of Independence stressed life, liberty, and the pursuit of happiness; accordingly, it shattered the notion of holding new territories in the subordinate status of colonies. The Northwest Ordinance of 1787 set forth a procedure for new states to enter the Union on an equal footing with the old. The Federal Constitution shortly confirmed this novel means of building a nation out of equal states. The step-by-step process through which territories have achieved self-government and national representation is among the most important of the Founding Fathers' legacies.

The method of state-making reconciled the ancient conflict between liberty and empire, resulting in what Thomas Jefferson called an empire for liberty. The system has worked and remains unaltered, despite enormous changes that have taken place in the nation. The country's extent and variety now surpass anything the patriots of '76 could likely have imagined. The United States has changed from an agrarian republic into a highly industrial and urban democracy, from a fledgling nation into a major world power. As Oliver Wendell Holmes remarked in 1920, the creators of the nation could not have seen completely how it and its constitution and its states would develop. Any meaningful review in the bicentennial era must consider what the country has become, as well as what it was.

The new nation of equal states took as its motto *E Pluribus Unum*—"out of many, one." But just as many peoples have become Americans without complete loss of ethnic and cultural identities, so have the states retained differences of character. Some have been superficial, expressed in stereotyped images— big, boastful Texas, "sophisticated" New York, "hillbilly" Arkansas. Other differences have been more real, sometimes instructively, sometimes amusingly; democracy has embraced Huey Long's Louisiana, bilingual New Mexico, unicameral Nebraska, and a Texas that once taxed fortunetellers and spawned politicians called "Woodpecker Republicans" and "Skunk Democrats." Some differences have been profound, as when South Carolina secessionists led other states out of the Union in opposition to abolitionists in Massachusetts and Ohio. The result was a bitter Civil War.

The Revolution's first shots may have sounded in Lexington and Concord; but fights over what democracy should mean and who should have independence have erupted from Pennsylvania's Gettysburg to the "Bleeding Kansas" of John Brown, from the Alamo in Texas to the Indian battles at Montana's Little Bighorn. Utah Mormons have known the strain of isolation; Hawaiians at Pearl Harbor, the terror of attack; Georgians during Sherman's march, the sadness of defeat and devastation. Each state's experience differs instructively; each adds understanding to the whole.

The purpose of this series of books is to make that kind of understanding accessible, in a way that will last in value far beyond the bicentennial fireworks. The series offers a volume on every state, plus the District of Columbia—fifty-one, in all.

Each book contains, besides the text, a view of the state through eyes other than the author's—a "photographer's essay," in which a skilled photographer presents his own personal perceptions of the state's contemporary flavor.

We have asked authors not for comprehensive chronicles, nor for research monographs or new data for scholars. Bibliographies and footnotes are minimal. We have asked each author for a summing up—interpretive, sensitive, thoughtful, individual, even personal—of what seems significant about his or her state's history. What distinguishes it? What has mattered about it, to its own people and to the rest of the nation? What has it come to now?

To interpret the states in all their variety, we have sought a variety of backgrounds in authors themselves and have encouraged variety in the approaches they take. They have in common only these things: historical knowledge, writing skill, and strong personal feelings about a particular state. Each has wide latitude for the use of the short space. And if each succeeds, it will be by offering you, in your capacity as a *citizen* of a state *and* of a nation, stimulating insights to test against your own.

James Morton Smith
General Editor

Preface

N books which deal with history, a preface is the author's only moment alone with the reader before leaving a book to be judged on its own. This is the appropriate place to acknowledge debts incurred in the process of writing. Here is an opportunity to court the reader's sympathy by hinting at hardships surmounted and rigors endured to bring the task to completion. The preface offers a chance to explain what sort of book was contemplated and seek to wheedle the reader into a receptive mood. This author intends to take full advantage of the broad license afforded by a preface.

This is a volume in a series of state histories published to mark the bicentennial. Authors were requested to keep within limited space, necessitating a choice between attempting to compress the entire history of a state into less than two hundred pages or choosing to concentrate on selected aspects. I have chosen to write selectively rather than to attempt an abridged treatment such as that employed in encyclopedias.

This choice was not dictated solely by limitations of space. The editors of this series requested a somewhat different kind of history from the standard chronological account offered by most textbooks or from the learned discourses found in academic journals. They invited authors to reflect upon the mind, spirit, and outlook which distinguish citizens of one state from those of another. I have sought to respond to their invitation "to think about a state one cares about'' and even to venture personal impressions, thereby entering perilous terrain where prudent historians seldom venture. In their charge to writers, the editors also beckoned them to blow fresh air into state history by searching hitherto neglected nooks and crannies of the past or bringing newer historical theories to the fore. Textbooks and chronological accounts being readily available, the editors of this series sought interpretive essays rather than the more traditional approach.

Authors were also urged to complete their work within the span of one year so that the volumes could be published before the rosy glow of the bicentennial had faded. This is not to suggest that this topic has engaged my attention only for that brief span of time. I have been an Alabamian since early childhood. My formal education took place in this state. Like most Alabamians, I prize a sense of belonging here. In teaching history, I have sought insight into the very subject to which this volume is addressed, the distinctive characteristics of Alabamians. In the years which I have spent in college classrooms, my students have probably taught me much more about the nature of Alabamians than I have been able to teach them about the history of the United States. The invitation to participate in this series was a challenge I could not resist.

But those readers who want a comprehensive treatment of Alabama history must look elsewhere. Neither space nor time nor the concept of this series allowed for a comprehensive piece of work. Those who prefer their history presented in neat chronological sequence should turn to textbooks or to more conventional works. Fellow academicians who may be disturbed by the sparsity of footnotes and the brevity of the suggestions for further reading should understand that this series is addressed primarily to lay readers rather than to scholars who demand documentation for every fact and complete bibliographical data. This book contains a limited number of footnotes and an abbreviated reading list but obviously I owe unacknowledged debts to many other sources.

In the months during which I have been obsessed by this assignment, I have been sustained by the forbearance of my family and of my husband in particular. I am especially indebted to Dean George Passey of the School of Social and Behavioral Sciences of the University of Alabama in Birmingham for allowing me the freedom to arrange my schedule so that I could shoulder this project along with my responsibilities to the university. In an effort to share my burden with fellow scholars, I inveigled a number of academic colleagues into reading and reacting to my work in progress. They are not to be held accountable for errors this book may contain or for my interpretations, but the following persons have read portions of this essay and contributed to any merit which is to be found within its pages: Dr. Leah R. Atkins, Dr. Hugh C. Bailey, Dr. William D. Barnard, Ms. Ann Boucher, Dr. Blaine A. Brownell, Dr. Wayne Flynt, Dr. David E. Harrell, Jr., Dr. Jack D. L. Holmes, Dr. Edward S. LaMonte, Dr. Melton McLaurin, Dr. Roger Nance, Dr. Ernest Porterfield, Dr. George P. Rawick, Dr. Robert Reid, and George R. Stewart. Two nonprofessional historians, Carl Elliott and Thad Holt, also read excerpts. I am indebted to my students Brenda Bodine, Yvonne Crumpler, and James Lopez for research assistance and to my patient typists Brenda Herron and Jeanette Teal for enduring what must have seemed endless revisions. Gerald George, managing editor of the Bicentennial State Histories, has been consistently supportive, even while exhorting the writers of fifty-one books to produce their best possible work at the fastest possible speed.

Virginia Van der Veer Hamilton

July 1976

Alabama

1

Shades of Ma and Pa:
The Obscured Ancestors

ALABAMA was conceived in a folk migration which would not be exceeded until the Forty-Niners stampeded to California. Gripped by "Alabama fever" which broke out following the War of 1812, pioneers streamed out of the valley of Virginia and the piedmont of the Carolinas and Georgia in such numbers that travellers headed north on these forest pathways were never out of sight of wagon trains of settlers hurrying to take over the last great Indian hunting ground east of the Mississippi.[1] Many migrants trudged afoot, their wagons packed with children and rude possessions. At the close of a day's weary journey, Sara Jane Lide of South Carolina wrote in her diary: "Got along very badly today. Roads rough and muddy, my oxen give out and little waggon [sic] broke down."[2] An English geographer who encountered 1,200 such travellers within a single day was reminded of a biblical exodus "except for the decided style of cursing and swearing."[3]

Born of the same restless, vital urge which was to people

1. A.B. Moore, *History of Alabama* (Tuscaloosa: Alabama Book Store, 1951), p. 75.

2. Lucille Griffith, *Alabama: A Documentary History to 1900*, rev. ed. (University, Ala.: University of Alabama Press, 1972), p. 138.

3. Walter B. Posey, *Alabama in the 1830s As Recorded by British Travelers* (Birmingham: Birmingham-Southern College, 1938), p. 30.

Texas, the Great Plains, and California, Alabama lost sight of her frontier heritage when she strayed up the narrow fork of secession. Although the wagon train became a cherished image west of the Mississippi River, it vanished from collective memory in Alabama amidst the smoke and flame of civil war. Pioneers in buckskins and linsey-woolsey were no match for the allure of Old Master and Mistress, their son the Confederate Hero, and their daughter the Southern Belle. Log cabin imagery gradually disappeared but the specter of the Big House rose like some phoenix from the ashes to dominate the landscape of Alabama history.

Against the backdrop of this stately mansion, generations of white Alabamians, costumed in Confederate uniforms and elaborate hoopskirts, sought to re-enact the halcyon days of the plantation. Searching will books and moldy gravestones, they hoped to encounter those elusive ancestors, the blue-blooded Virginians, surveying acres of cotton and choruses of slaves from their broad veranda. But this quest led more often to the dogtrot of a cabin in the Alabama wilderness, where sat Ma and Pa from Georgia, the Carolina piedmont, or the mountains of Tennessee, watching a passel of kids, chickens, cats, and dogs kick up dust in the bare front yard.

One descendant of Alabama pioneers, schooled in plantation imagery, had to go as far away as the University of Chicago to discover that his native piedmont, like Albemarle County, where some of Thomas Jefferson's democratic notions were nourished, was once a part of the American West and to feel pride in that heritage. "This new learning was good for my soul," Herman C. Nixon reflected later, "and I no longer had an occasional wish that my people might have been planters." [4]

Clarence Cason, a sensitive writer from the small piedmont town of Ragland, wondered if the persistent ethos of the plantation might be due to an obstinate preference by Alabamians for fiction over reality. Or if it could somehow be blamed on a "dreamy and miasmic mental lethargy," caused by malaria,

---

4. Herman C. Nixon, *Lower Piedmont Country*, American Folkway Series (1936; reprint ed., Freeport, N.Y.: Books for Libraries Press, 1971), p. xix.

hookworm, and heavy humidity.[5] Wilbur J. Cash suggested that plain folk were enthralled by their distant "cousinly" relationship with planters and by paternalism masked as kindness.[6] C. Vann Woodward theorized that planter and farmer, having suffered in the downfall of the Confederacy and the enforced reconstruction of their society, were bonded for generations by shared defeat and humiliation.[7]

There are other, less abstruse explanations for Alabama's neglect of a rightful heritage from the westward movement. The great majority of her twentieth-century citizens have been educated, not at some Yankee university but safely at home where many textbooks and local histories open with the matchless adventure of Hernando de Soto, linger fondly over antebellum life in the Black Belt, grieve for the Confederacy, and tend to regard events in the century following the Civil War as decidedly anticlimactic. The frontier saga has not only been smothered beneath pervasive legends of the plantation but starved for lack of its own published history. Writers bold enough to criticize the dominance of planters and industrialists have found it necessary to brace themselves for an onslaught of what Cash called the "Savage Ideal," the tendency of a "techy" society to harry nonconformists out of its bosom.

But recently there has been a slow and subtle shifting of the wind. Descendants of Alabama pioneers have begun to revive the old skills, crafts, and music of their ancestors, restore some of their simple cabins, grist mills, stores, and log churches, and preserve almost forgotten annals of the plain people of rural communities. By so doing, Carl Elliott learned the simple chronicle of his great-grandfather Hezekiah Massey, brought to Alabama at the age of nine by parents from North Carolina who had never seen a train and did not know "a letter in the book." Hezekiah was to live a long and self-reliant pastoral existence in

5. Clarence Cason, *90° in the Shade* (Chapel Hill, N.C.: University of North Carolina Press, 1935), p. 52.

6. See Wilbur J. Cash, *The Mind of the South* (New York: Alfred A. Knopf, 1941).

7. This is one of the themes examined in C. Vann Woodward, *The Burden of Southern History* (Baton Rouge: Louisiana State University Press, 1960; New York: Vintage Books, Alfred A. Knopf, 1960).

Pickens County, depending almost exclusively upon his own crops and razorback hogs to feed a burgeoning family. In old age he liked to boast that he had never bought a bushel of corn and only sixteen pounds of meat.[8]

Obeying the biblical injunction to multiply and replenish the earth, Hezekiah and his wife, Margaret, had twelve children, nearly a hundred grandchildren, and before they died had met their first fifty great-grandchildren, including Carl Elliott, who served for a time in Congress. Their descendants apparently enjoyed and esteemed them, hordes gathering at their country home every Fourth of July. Endowed with good health, Hezekiah put in a crop every year until he was eighty-six; Margaret walked four miles when she was eighty-two to visit a son. Hezekiah saw a train but never rode one, evidently feeling no need to leave home.

Yet admirable pioneers such as these have been slighted and demeaned during the century in which Alabama historiography has focused almost obsessively upon the cult of plantation and Confederacy. The budding of folk history is a healthy sign. If it continues to flower, the majority of white Alabamians may someday be purged of a lingering regret that their forebears were not planters.

Collectors of family annals should be wary, however, lest they embrace a new set of myths. As they divest themselves of the notion that they are heirs to the plantation, they need not rush to the opposite extreme of envisioning ancestors from that frequently scorned and ridiculed caste called "hillbillies," "clay eaters," "piney woods folks," or "po' white trash." Although Alabama had its share of this unfortunate fringe of society, the "po' white trash," reduced to indolence by hookworm, malnutrition, illiteracy, and despair, probably did not exceed 20 percent of the antebellum white population of the South.

It is far likelier that a twentieth-century Alabamian's forebears belonged to the much more numerous antebellum category designated by historians as yeomen, middle-class, or simply

---

8. Carl Elliott, comp., *Annals of Northwest Alabama,* 4 vols. (Tuscaloosa: privately printed, 1958), 1:207–208.

"plain folk." Like Hezekiah and Margaret Massey, most of these small farmers owned their own land, tilled the soil themselves, concentrating more upon raising foodstuffs for their families than cotton for the market, and came to have a deep sense of independence and self-reliance.

Although they owned few slaves, if any, the overwhelming majority of these yeomen fought for the Confederacy. Yet Alabamians, accustomed to thinking of Confederate loyalty in their state as monolithic, are sometimes surprised to discover forebears who donned the Confederate gray only reluctantly, deserted the Southern cause, or even served in the Union army.

Glancing back at the political heritage of their ancestors, folk historians might well be skeptical of the old saw that Grandpa always voted the straight Democratic ticket. In the antebellum era many humble folk belonged to the Whig party, although Democrats were generally stronger in the pine barrens, hills, and scrub lands. During the 1890s plain citizens erupted in angry revolt against the Democratic leadership and would have seated a party rebel in the governor's chair had their votes been fairly counted. To envision all the ancestors as stubborn conservatives is also risky. The odds are strong that many of one's forebears wore wool hats, took part in turbulent movements such as the Grange, the Farmers' Alliance, or a brand of Populism known as "Jeffersonian Democrats," and in their day were considered radicals.

To visualize ancestors who were unfailingly sober is to ignore countless anecdotes about heavy consumption of alcohol during the first third of the nineteenth century. In later eras and despite laws to the contrary, the old folks were prone to concoct their own brand of spirits by the light of the moon and to secrete jugs of corn liquor in their barns. Although they have traditionally displayed warm hospitality to strangers whom they instinctively trusted and although most became fervent converts to Methodism or the Baptist faith, it is necessary to face the unpleasant truth that these same folk spawned numbers of racists, nativists, religious bigots, lynchers, and Klansmen.

In the old pioneer art of quilting, a coverlet of clashing colors and varying shapes, made from any scraps which might be at hand, was called a "crazy quilt." The plain folk themselves often appeared to be a patchwork of contradictory qualities, kindness and cruelty, Puritanism and hedonism, a deep-rooted work ethic and a capacity for leisure, radicalism and conservatism, nationalism and sectionalism. As they struggled to survive the harsh experiences of pioneering, agrarianism, poverty, exploitation, civil war, and racial strife, Ma and Pa pieced their own "crazy quilt" of contrary elements. They have bequeathed this vivid heirloom to their descendants.

Among the first white folk to claim land in this new Southwest after 1814 were Indian fighters who had served as privates in Andrew Jackson's militia, broken the spirited Creeks, and forced them to cede twenty million choice acres including the heartland of present-day Alabama. The Looney brothers, Henry and Jack, who fought at the climactic battle of Horseshoe Bend, then returned to Tennessee to fetch their parents and migrate to what is now the piedmont county of St. Clair, were typical of such men.[9] So were the four Mahan brothers, Irish by ancestry and blacksmiths by profession, who discovered Alabama in Jackson's ranks and came back to settle on the site of a deserted Indian village beside a creek in present-day Bibb County. Blacksmiths, machinists, and wagonmakers from Jackson's brigades remained in north Alabama to shoe horses, mules, or oxen and make the shovels, axes, plowtips, cook pans, and dog irons so vital to pioneers.[10]

Militiamen were followed by farmers from the older piedmont who sought to better their lot and were ambitious enough to uproot their families for the long trek toward an uncertain future. Redding Byrd travelled for a month by wagon and horse cart to bring his large family from North Carolina to that area in southeastern Alabama known as the wiregrass. On land near present-day Ozark, his eight sons cleared a few acres and sowed

9. Mattie Lou Teague Crow, *History of St. Clair County (Alabama)* (Huntsville: Strode Publishers, 1973), p. 24.

10. Ethel Armes, *The Story of Coal and Iron in Alabama* (1910; reprint ed., Birmingham: Book-keepers Press, 1972), pp. 2, 24.

their first corn crop.[11] Highland Scots, bearing the names of old clans like the McRaes, McDonalds, McSweans, and McInnises, left the inhospitable Cape Fear region of North Carolina and moved to the Pea River in southeastern Alabama where they comprised a community known as "little Scotland." [12] Deep in the Great Smoky Mountains, Ira Harmon and his family heard of more fertile land, rode a flatboat down the Nolichucky, Holston, and Tennessee rivers, toted their sparse household goods overland to the Oostanaula, made another flatboat, floated downstream to the Coosa, and followed that river until coming to shore in Talladega County. If lucky or clever, a farmer might become a planter in time; if less fortunate and not so pushy, he remained a small farmer; if a loser in the land grab, he moved his family further west or, drifting into a condition of hopelessness, descended to the bottom rail of poor whites.

On clear mornings Alabama hills reverberated to the thump of axes girdling trees for pasture or felling them for cabins. The Looney brothers squared the logs of their two-story house near Ashville so precisely that there were no cracks between the timbers, erected twin chimneys of hard-pressed pink brick, built a staircase which would still be sturdy a century and half later, and with a hot poker burned the date 1820 into a corner log.

But others in their haste for shelter made what the Yankee observer Frederick Law Olmsted described as "rude log huts" about fifteen feet square, with dirt floors, a single window, and what were known as "Alabama bedsteads," pallets of broom sage, crabgrass, or corn shucks put atop rough frames fitted into cracks in two walls and supported by a single corner pole. A fireplace of bricks or wooden slats plastered with mud served for heating and cooking.[13] Arriving at such a home at the end of

---

11. W.L. Andrews, "Early History of Southeast Alabama," *Alabama Historical Quarterly* 10 (1948): 106.

12. Anne Kendrick Walker, *Backtracking in Barbour County: A Narrative of the Last Alabama Frontier* (Richmond: Dietz Press, 1941), p. 112.

13. Frederick Law Olmsted, *A Journey in the Back Country,* Sourcebooks in Negro History (1860; reprint ed., New York: Schocken Books, 1970), p. 205; Wesley S. Thompson, *The Free State of Winston: A History of Winston County, Alabama* (Winfield, Ala.: Pareil Press, 1968), pp. 150–151.

her long wagon journey from South Carolina, one pioneer wife, accustomed to more comfort, dissolved in hysteria. E. A. Powell of Tuscaloosa County was only a young boy at the time but he never forgot his mother's grief. "She just let go," he recalled.[14]

Migrants like the Byrds, Harmons, Looneys, and Mahans could scarcely aspire to own acreage in the only areas of Alabama then considered prime cotton land, the rich bottoms of the Tennessee, Tombigbee, and Alabama rivers and that crescent of fertile land which curved through south central Alabama like a new moon and came to be known as the Black Belt. Around Huntsville, fertile land which yielded a thousand pounds of cotton to the acre had been claimed before 1805 by well-to-do settlers of English ancestry with the means to pay $50 to $100 an acre, build fine brick houses instead of log cabins, and amuse themselves by racing fast horses like the famous Gray Gander, betting on cockfights, and living, so the traveller Anne Royall found, "in great splendor." [15] Some uppity residents wanted to call their town Twickenham after the country home of the British poet Alexander Pope. But fortunately sensible citizens prevailed, selecting a more appropriate name to honor the pioneer John Hunt, who operated a castor oil shop and had killed the rattlesnakes around Big Spring as early as 1805 by exploding gunpowder in the rock fissures.

Huntsville, which became temporary capital of the new state in 1819, thrived on cotton, slavery, and river transportation. In this first year of Alabama's statehood, a clerk at the Green Bottom Inn was startled to be confronted by a stranger requesting lodging and identifying himself as president of the United States. James Monroe, curious about the booming new Southwest, had come unannounced and accompanied only by an army lieutenant and a male secretary. Residents hastily arranged a dinner to welcome the distinguished visitor to "our remote and humble village." One orator on this occasion addressed Monroe as "Your Excellency," but a Huntsville newspaper made note

14. Griffith, *Alabama,* p. 137.
15. Griffith, *Alabama,* p. 180.

of the fact that even haughty residents were pleased because the president had appeared among them as a plain citizen.[16]

Rich land along the Alabama River was sold at Milledgeville, Georgia, mainly to speculators. Sales later took place at the land office in Cahaba, deep within the Black Belt and far from pioneer trails. But coves and tableland in the hill country could be bought at Huntsville for as little as $1.25 an acre unless, as often happened, speculators bid against squatters who had improved their lands and thereby forced them to pay higher prices. Many settlers actually preferred the hills because they were familiar with the terrain, found the climate more invigorating and healthier than that of the lowlands, and relished the freestone water which flowed from numerous springs.[17] The soil itself was a practical reason for settling in the highlands. Men who guided their own plowboards could till sandy soil themselves whereas it required gangs of slaves, fearful of the whip, to clear and work the gummy clay of the Black Belt.

Unlike lowland planters who sometimes plowed up corn to make room for cotton when the price of the money crop was high, hill farmers looked upon corn as their major crop and raised cotton as a sideline. In 1860 only 352 bales of cotton were produced in the hill county of Winston, a figure 1/180th of the cotton production that same year in the Black Belt county of Dallas. Farmers raised sorghum, peas, potatoes, and beans, experimented with tobacco, oats, rye, or barley, allowed their razorbacks and lean cattle to forage in the woods, and like Hezekiah Massey were accustomed to providing their own sustenance. Independent and self-reliant, the majority of small farmers stuck to the uplands or the wiregrass, although even blacks jeered at them: "You can't raise cotton on sandy lan'; I'd ruther be a nigger than a po' white man." [18]

Like most jeers this one was too broad for accuracy. Al-

16. Griffith, *Alabama*, pp. 66–68.

17. Donald B. Dodd and Wynelle S. Dodd, *Winston: An Antebellum and Civil War History of a Hill County of North Alabama; Annals of Northwest Alabama,* 4 vols. (Birmingham: Oxmoor Press, 1972), 4: 20–31.

18. Nixon, *Lower Piedmont Country,* p. 10.

though swindled by speculators, forced to "make do" with the leavings of the great land sales, to till thin soils in the hill country or plow the less fertile land which adjoined the choice holdings of lowland planters, most pioneers achieved the goal for which they had migrated westward on the forest paths. By 1860 eighty percent of the yeoman farmers of Alabama owned the land they tilled.

The great Appalachian mountain chain, dwindling to foothills and piedmont, penetrates northeastern Alabama like a wedge. While farmers wrestled infertile soil and existed at nature's mercy, plain folk of more imaginative cast of mind dug beneath this highland crust to discover its real wealth—beds of coal and the great ore range of the South. Indians had known of the famous Red Mountain of north Alabama, ninety miles long, a mile wide at places, and three hundred feet high, and had come from as far away as Mississippi to fetch its rock for war paint and dyeing. Pioneers, too, stained their fingers when they touched the red rock but concluded that it had no use other than to dye jeans, breeches, blankets, and linsey dresses. Finding local ore too brittle to hammer on their anvils, blacksmiths imported bar iron from hundreds of miles away. But Sir Charles Lyell, the English geologist, noted as early as 1846 that iron and limestone lay adjacent to great beds of coal in Roupes Valley between present-day Birmingham and Tuscaloosa and realized what such a combination could portend. Invited to admire the dark, rich soil of the Black Belt, the geologist startled an acquaintance in Selma by predicting that the real wealth of Alabama lay in the north.

Farmers avoided these mineral lands or sold them. One disposed of a rocky patch near Russellville to Col. Enoch Ensley for fifty dollars; in time that ten-acre tract would come to be regarded as one of the richest possessions of Sloss Sheffield Coal and Iron Company. The Reverend R. K. Hargrove, a Methodist preacher, once passed up a chance to buy the whole of Red Mountain from present-day Trussville to Bessemer for $30,000.

Although blacksmiths failed to mold the iron, more sophisticated ironmakers succeeded. Twelve years before the first cotton cloth mill in Alabama was built, Joseph Heslip, an ironmonger, bought land in a bend of Cedar Creek near Russellville for two dollars an acre and built in 1818 the first blast furnace in the state, a rough limestone structure constructed after the style of furnaces built by ancient Britons and Romans. In Roupes Valley around 1830, Daniel Hillman, an old Dutch furnaceman from Pennsylvania, erected his forge beside a rushing creek and rich pockets of brown ore. After Hillman's death, the furnace was bought by a cotton planter, Ninion Tannehill, whose name it bears today. Along the creeks of Bibb and Shelby counties, the Mahans and others erected forges, bloomeries, and furnaces and began to make farm implements, cookware, and washpots from Alabama ore. Enterprising ironmakers raised $2,500 to $3,000 to start in business in Calhoun, Talladega, and Cherokee counties.

Thousands of cedars were cut and burned to make the charcoal to fire these furnaces. Water-powered bellows furnished the blast necessary to lift the huge cast iron hammer which fell of its own weight over molten iron. Such hammers weighed 500 to 600 pounds, but workers at Cane Creek furnace in Calhoun County boasted that a man of giant stature once lifted their hammer from its anvil. Hammers rose and fell eighty strokes a minute, their steady throb audible for four to five miles on still days. The Riddle brothers of Pennsylvania, who forged iron at Maria forge in Talladega County, proudly stamped their product with a boar's head crest and claimed that it equalled the finest ore of Sweden.

Crude though this ironmaking process was, it was more complex than that by which Alabama coal was first mined. David Hanby, who had been a machinist for Jackson, raised coal from the bed of the Warrior River by anchoring a flatboat over the seam and loosening the coal with crowbars driven into a ledge. Divers working in pairs went down to grasp the coal and load it on a boat. This product, called stonecoal to distinguish it from charcoal, was received with doubt when Hanby shipped it to

Mobile for sale. He had to give it away at first, sending a black boy with every bucketful to demonstrate how it could be lighted and burned.

Vigorous entrepreneurs like Daniel Hillman, Joseph Heslip, and David Hanby were precursors of the big industrialists to come. But others who mined the mineral resources were described by contemporary observer Mary Gordon Duffee as "a peculiar type of simple-minded humanity" who lived off patches of corn, peas, and yams and dug coal only if it was "handy to git at." After trading a wagonload of coal for a luxury such as corn liquor, these "coal haulers," prostrate in the beds of their wagons, relied on their oxen to find the way home unaided.[19]

In creeks and rivers of Walker County, flatboats were loaded with coal in summer when the water was low and floated downstream in winter or spring when the tide rose. It took an expert river pilot to bring flatboat, crew, and coal safely through the dreaded Squaw Shoals of the Warrior River above Tuscaloosa or to transport iron from the Talladega Mountains over the terrifying "devil's staircase" where the Coosa dashed through rapids, narrows, and rocks on its way to Wetumpka. Boatmen became folk heroes who were reputed to walk ninety miles home in two days and whose devil-may-care attitude toward a perilous profession is hinted in this folk song:

> Oh! Dance, boatman, dance
> Oh! Dance, boatman, dance
> Dance all night til broad daylight
> And go home with the girls in the morning.[20]

Coal and iron were boated out of the mountains because Alabama, lagging far behind other southern states, had only 165 miles of railroad track as late as 1852. Ironmasters of isolated little furnaces could not mount a united protest and would have made small impact in any case, their trade being considered

19. Mary Gordon Duffee, *Sketches of Alabama*, eds., Virginia Pounds Brown and Jane Porter Nabers (University, Ala.: University of Alabama Press, 1970), p. 48.
20. Duffee, *Sketches*, p. 12. Used by permission.

useful only as it served the dominant agricultural interests. Cotton was the proper and most profitable pursuit of gentlemen; all others were shunted aside as ruffians or backwoodsmen. In the entire mineral district before the Civil War, only seventeen forges, nine primitive furnaces, and one crude rolling mill were engaged in ironmaking. In Jefferson County, which would be the center of a great postwar industrial boom, a few smiths hammered iron by hand.

War gave the incipient industry a prestige and purpose it had theretofore lacked. The onetime Union frigate *Merrimac* had been converted into the Confederate ironclad *Virginia* with the help of iron from Cane Creek furnace; the famous Brooke cannon of Selma were cast from Alabama iron. But most impressive of all to Confederates was the performance of their ironclad, the *Tennessee,* plated at Selma with three layers of iron from Shelby County. Before surrendering in the battle for Mobile Bay, the *Tennessee* stood off the firepower of seventeen federal vessels without a single shell penetrating her armor. When the war came to its end, shrewd men, both Southern and Northern, were ready to look more closely into the possibilities for mining fortunes from the resources of the mineral region.

Alabama pioneers venerated rugged individuals like "Andy" Jackson and "Davy" Crockett, fancying themselves as cut from the same heroic pattern. Yet they were more dependent upon family and neighbors than would be their great-grandchildren dwelling in cities. How could timber be moved to create farmland unless a dozen or more men, working as "toting partners," placed poles under a heavy log, lifted in unison, and, straining leg muscles to the utmost, stood erect and marched to the edge of the field? How could a house be raised in a day or a hundred bushels of corn shucked in an evening without the help of every able-bodied male within a radius of five miles? When woods were burned over each autumn, how could the fire be kept under control unless the whole neighborhood turned out to beat down random flames with pine brushes? How tedious to piece a quilt if there were no lively gossip around its edges and no sips of rum toddy or wine to make the fingers move faster.

Forced to co-operate in order to survive, pioneers demon-strated their prowess as "he men" or let off steam in strenuous competition. One partner on the end of a logrolling pole might secretly hope that the other would fail to stand up so that he could "h'ist" the heavy burden unaided. Males coveted the repu-tation of being able to "pull down" any man in the community in a log tote. During breaks in the rolling they raced or wres-tled, a small man with sinews like steel cables sometimes "pull-ing down" a muscular two-hundred-pounder. At corn shuck-ings, teams competed to see which could shuck the highest pile, the evening often ending in a raucous corncob battle.[21]

Homemade liquor, an unquestioned necessity of pioneer life, enlivened all community events, flowing in greatest abundance on election day. E. A. Powell, a folk historian, remembered that bottles of whiskey, brandy, rum, and wine, with a can-didate's name on each, stretched the entire length of the dry goods store in a typical little northwest Alabama community. Militia musters often ended in drunken brawls, officers and privates forgetting all distinctions of rank. After a new cabin was raised, workers celebrated by consuming a keg of whiskey and riding their host on a rail. On quiet nights in the hills, the shouts of singers at a corn shucking could be heard for miles, their leader exhorting "pull off the shucks, boys, pull off the shucks"; then "give me a dram, sir, give me a dram." [22]

Oldtimers could not recall ever contemplating an eventuality such as prohibition in the 1820s and 1830s when every inn-keeper advertised peach brandy, rum, wine, and corn whiskey at twelve and a half to thirty-seven and a half cents a gulp, plus the necessary sequel of lodging for the night. No food was served in taverns known as "doggeries" but liquor flowed so abundantly that drunken patrons quarrelled and fought. Corn liquor is not called "white lightnin' " and "white mule" with-out good reason; it has its own mystique, deserving of its repute

21. Mitchell B. Garrett, *Horse and Buggy Days on Hatchet Creek* (University, Ala.: University of Alabama Press, 1957), pp. 216–218; Frank L. Owsley, *Plain Folk of the Old South* (Baton Rouge: Louisiana State University Press, 1948), p. 108.
22. Dodd, *Winston,* p. 60.

as a cure for snakebites, a searing draught for "roping" coffee on winter mornings or killing the "bugs" in a drink of river water, and powerful enough "to make a rabbit spit in a bulldog's face." Persuaded to sample it during the 1920s, the New York writer Carl Carmer found this homemade whiskey "as vile and uglily potent a liquor as ever man has distilled." [23]

Although Alabama had dry spells early in the twentieth century, moonshining and drinking went on apace. When Hugo Black's older brother Pelham drowned after his buggy overturned in a creek, it was whispered in Ashland that Pelham had been on a drinking spree in defiance of the teaching of his Baptist father. Herman Nixon remembered that farmers, fearful of the wrath of their wives, hid their bottles in trees and barns, and he described an ingenious service rendered by a Bluffton merchant known as "Bell Tree" Smith. Customers placed money in a box under a tree, rang a bell, and discreetly retired from sight. When the bell again sounded, the purchaser found his money gone and a bottle in the box. But many a resident of Nixon's home community of Possum Trot burned to death while drinking alone or, attempting to stagger home, fell under a freight train or froze in an open field.

No wonder that preachers like the mountain evangelist Sam Jones thundered against "devil rum," drummed out of the fellowship those unlucky enough to be caught drunk, and urged their congregations to press for Prohibition as social reform, or that John T. Triggs, a Methodist "gospel ranger," reported that settlers in some rural areas of southeast Alabama were "hardened in wickedness." [24] Uninhibited use of strong liquor threatened the stability and cohesion upon which rural people relied for their very survival. Drinking was castigated from the pulpit along with such capers as gambling, horseracing, theater, and dancing (damned by Sam Jones as "huggin' set to music") [25] enjoyed by the elite of more permissive faiths.

23. Carl Carmer, *Stars Fell on Alabama* (New York: Farrar and Rinehart, 1934), p. 7.

24. Fred S. Watson, *Forgotten Trails: A History of Dale County, Alabama 1824–1966*, ed. William R. Snell (Birmingham, Ala.: Bonner Press, 1968), p. 163.

25. Nixon, *Lower Piedmont Country*, p. 85.

Mount Zion Baptist Church of Springville struck from its rolls unrepentant brethren and sisters guilty of "falsety and delaying payment, use of ill language, trading on the Sabbath, communing with a church of another denomination, horseracing, dancing, and talking two ways," [26] a catechism of sins which, if enforced as grounds for expulsion, would empty many a modern congregation. When "stars" fell on Alabama one November night in 1833, those engaged in drinking or dancing believed that these meteorites had been hurled from the armory of an angry God. At protracted meetings that winter many a penitent came forward.

Rude log churches and brush arbors, offering scant protection from sun, rain, or chill, sheltered the spiritual yearnings of plain folk. Although worshippers came primarily in search of religious solace, churchgoing served them also as a social, political, and commercial clearing house and gave them a rare taste of oratory, stagecraft, literature, and exaltation.[27] C. C. "Buddy" Collins of Winston County was said to be so eloquent that he could "touch the dead corpse of a protracted meeting and it would spring to its feet a revival." [28] Sam Jones took his time in arousing a crowd, explaining candidly: "I never kill hogs 'til I get the water hot." [29] The Reverend John Powers threatened congregations in the Pinson area of Jefferson County: "If I cannot by entreaty and prayers and tears melt your wicked souls, I ought to thrash saving grace into your sinful bodies." [30]

After vividly describing hell's fire, a revivalist might call for the hymn, "Almost Persuaded," stirring his listeners to tears for the fate of those who failed to come to the mourners' bench before its concluding words, "almost, but lost." In antebellum times a funeral sermon might be delivered weeks late because no Methodist preacher was at hand. But when the circuit rider

26. Crow, *St. Clair County*, p. 114.

27. Cason, *90° in the Shade*, pp. 66–67; Dickson D. Bruce, Jr., *And They All Sang Hallelujah: Plain Folk Camp Meeting Religion* (Knoxville: University of Tennessee Press, 1973) is a perceptive study of frontier religion.

28. Dodd, *Winston*, p. 51.

29. Nixon, *Lower Piedmont Country*, p. 85.

30. Duffee, *Sketches*, p. 45.

hove into view, hordes of the curious convened to hear his verdict as to whether the departed was enjoying the pleasures of heaven or suffering the torments of hell.

People of the Alabama hills and piedmont had little contact with "popish" Episcopalians or Roman Catholics and virtually none with such Yankee intellectuals as Congregationalists, Universalists, and Unitarians. Even Presbyterianism, with its educated ministers concerned over theological niceties, lost its initial headstart on the frontier to evangelical Baptists and Methodists who preached to plain folk in words they could understand, allowed worshippers to unwind in emotional shouting and song, and reassured members of both denominations in their frontier conviction that they were masters of their fate and guardians of their own salvation.

The majority of Alabama plain folk followed such evangels into the Methodist or Baptist faith, except for Primitive Baptists, who clung stoutly to the Calvinistic concept that the saved and the damned had been predestined and who practiced footwashing. Mitchell B. Garrett, the son of a Primitive Baptist preacher, spent many a Sunday morning in church at Hatchet Creek in Clay County and concurred with Carl Carmer as to the gist of a typical sermon. Attempting to reproduce "the blessed tone" which brought amens and shouts of encouragement from the congregation, Garrett added "ahs" to certain words for emphasis and rhythm. Such a sermon might continue for two hours but the heart of it went something like this:

> On the Resurrection Day-ah God's elected will stand on his right hand-ah and rejoice-ah while the wicked shall groan forever-ah in the torturin' flames of Hell-ah, Then us-ah that believe ever' word of the Bible-ah, us that's been buried in baptism-ah accordin' to the only right way-ah, us that knows the Lord's Supper-ah and washin' of the saints' feet-ah was meant to be carried on-ah, us Primitive Baptists-ah, will stand-ah and see judgment pronounced-ah on the dancin', card-playin' carnal sinners-ah. . . .[31]

Differences over predestination, free will, methods of baptism, or the question of whether women should speak in church

31. Garrett, *Horse and Buggy Days*, p. 175.

were topics of frequent and heated debate. But Methodists and Baptists, mingling, intermarrying, and producing more tolerant younger generations, came to view their dissimilarities with good humor, epitomized by the old story of a Baptist who claimed that his Methodist wife believed in falling from grace but never fell, while he, who believed there was no fall, fell every day.

However, those who propagated less familiar faiths courted actual danger. When two wandering Mormon elders sought converts in Clay County during the 1890s, Methodists, Baptists, and Primitive Baptists closed ranks to threaten the strangers with tarring and feathering. At the turn of the century, members of holiness and pentecostal sects were despised by Methodists and Baptists. Amid the nativist fervor of the 1920s, Catholic and Jewish minorities were often persecuted. In 1921 an itinerant Methodist preacher, angered because his daughter had married a Catholic, fatally shot the priest who had performed the ceremony. But the assailant was found "not guilty" by a jury in Birmingham, a city described by a national magazine of that era as "the American hot-bed of anti-Catholic fanaticism." [32]

For rural folk in pioneer times the great outdoor camp meeting, filled with emotion and song, was the pinnacle of each year, all other events being dated as taking place before or after this occasion. At China Grove in Dale County the annual gathering attracted five thousand, whose tents stretched a quarter of a mile in every direction. Held during the August recess between tilling and harvest known as "laying-by time," a camp meeting afforded rest from labor, the opportunity to hear several long sermons each day for two to three days, to mingle with strangers from neighboring states, and, if young, to court in the intoxicating atmosphere under the big brush arbors where hell-fire preachers declaimed, hymns surged, pine knot torches flickered, and sinners repented.

Cynics claimed that the camp meeting was no fit place for

32. Virginia V. Hamilton, *Hugo Black: The Alabama Years* (Baton Rouge: Louisiana State University Press, 1972), pp. 86–93.

young women because more souls were made there than saved. Yet the meeting offered a safety valve preferable to drinking, gambling, or brawling for the release of frontier tensions. At the climactic moment of the "altar call" the audience craned to watch normally decorous folk seized by uncontrollable "jerks" or "covaulting" in the throes of conversion. But Methodists and Baptists by the 1840s had gained so many converts that they had become established faiths. The camp meeting, having served the purposes of these evangelicals, began to fade from the rural scene, although its remnants could be found in northern Alabama until the First World War. Heralding a new religious wave, holiness and pentecostal sects took over many of the old campgrounds for their revivals.

Religion was central to the lives of Alabama pioneers who attended the little log churches, endured lengthy sermons from backless benches made of split timbers, followed song leaders who "h'isted" the tune and "lined out" white spirituals for those who could not read, and "pounded" their preachers at harvest time with homegrown staples, one Methodist flock in Cullman County presenting its leader with twenty gallons of molasses.[33] People of the hills, piney woods, and wiregrass looked forward to all-day singings, dinners on the ground, adorning their graveyards with flowers on Decoration Day in early summer, and gathering for a discordant and repetitious form of sixteenth-century chanting known as Sacred Harp. Mitchell Garrett described the four-note disharmony of Sacred Harp as bereft of melody or tune, filled with songs which sounded alike, and meant to be enjoyed by the singers but not necessarily by the audience.

Undoubtedly their religion filled a social need, served as an acceptable release for emotions, and gave these plain Alabamians a sense of self-esteem and mission. Within the church they found moments of orgiastic joy through music, prayer, testimonials, and repentance. Their preachers, focusing upon personal regeneration rather than social crusades, strove mightily to im-

33. Margaret Jean Jones, *Combing Cullman County* (Cullman, Ala.: Modernistic Printers, Inc., 1972), pp. 124–125.

plant in these congregations the desired Puritan values of hard work, self-reliance, education, sobriety, and abstention from sin. When rural folk began to move to cities filled with worldly temptations, they depended upon religion for reassurance, discipline, and a degree of community status.[34] (But many of these Puritans found the "vices" to be irresistibly attractive, if only from a distance.)

Even as they made strenuous efforts to follow the dictates of their preachers, many discovered again and again that fertile land, industrial wealth, higher education, political power, and other avenues of upward mobility were closed to them for reasons which they could not fathom. One scholar of the plain people's religion came to the poignant conclusion that "world rejection" was at the heart of frontier conversion.[35] Spiritual leaders had promised them that the virtuous, although poor and humble on earth, were to achieve the ultimate success, a place in heaven. But the faithful wondered, in the plaintive words of their old hymn, "How long, O Savior, O, how long?"

Some of the earliest Alabama pioneers had borne arms and earned bounty lands in the American Revolution. Having witnessed this momentous event or been personally involved in it, they named the town of Jasper for an obscure Revolutionary soldier; the counties of Washington, Sumter, St. Clair, Pickens, Morgan, Marion, DeKalb, and Greene for American generals; other counties in honor of the Marquis de Lafayette (Fayette) and of John Hancock, first signer of the Declaration of Independence.

During Alabama's formative period it seemed only fitting to name newly created counties for those who had helped scourge the Indians out of this abundant hunting ground (Dale, Butler, Clarke, Montgomery, Wilcox) and for heroes of the War of 1812 (Coffee, Perry, Pike, Covington, Lauderdale, Lawrence).[36] Successes in war imbued pioneers with respect for

34. Robert Coles, "God and The Rural Poor," *Psychology Today* 5 (1972): 31–41; Nixon, *Lower Piedmont Country*, pp. 92–94.

35. Bruce, *Camp Meeting Religion*, pp. 123–130.

36. Saffold Berney, *Hand-Book of Alabama* (Birmingham: Roberts and Sons, 1892), pp. 267–338; Elliott, comp., *Annals of Northwest Alabama*, 1:150.

the fighting strength of the Union. They became even further indebted to the federal government and to their old chieftain Andrew Jackson, whom they perceived as a champion of the common man for removing the Indians and opposing vested interests like the Bank of the United States. Long after the nationalistic spirit had waned in more populous areas, it remained strong among isolated people of the Alabama hills.

When Alabama was admitted to the Union in 1819, it was the eleventh slave state in a precarious national balancing act which would confront its first major challenge the next year. Issues of power in Washington seemed remote, however, to farmers preoccupied with elemental matters like rain and drought, planting and gathering. They bestirred themselves over such local political issues as whether the state capital should be located in the hills or near the coastal plain and how many representatives were allotted to them in the legislature. But quarrels over slavery were immaterial to most citizens of counties like Blount, Walker, and Hancock, which in 1850 comprised the bottom tier of Alabama's fifty-two counties in terms of slaveholding.

For every *one* slave in the combined area of Hancock, Walker, and Blount, there were *eighteen* in each of the Black Belt counties of Dallas, Greene, Marengo, and Montgomery. In Marion County the slave census of 1850 turned up only 856 slaves, almost one-sixth of them owned by two families, the Bankheads and the Hollises. Many a community of small farmers like Moody's Crossroads in St. Clair County contained not a single family which owned slaves. In some parts of the wiregrass the plantation system was similarly weak. On the eve of civil war there were only 314 slaveholders in a total white population of more than ten thousand in Dale County; in 1860 only Blount, Walker, and Winston counties had fewer slaves than Covington.[37]

Chapters of the American Colonization Society, which advocated that slaves, purchased from their owners, and free blacks be resettled in Africa, operated openly in north Alabama. James G. Birney, who was later to leave Alabama and become

---

37. Watson, *Forgotten Trails*, p. 54; Allen W. Jones, "Unionism and Disaffection in South Alabama: The Case of Alfred Holley," *Alabama Review* 24 (1971): 115.

presidential candidate of the Liberty party, represented Madison County in the Alabama legislature for a time and persuaded that body to include provision for manumission of slaves in the state constitution. But by opening fire on the "peculiar institution" abolitionists helped kill the antislavery movement in Alabama, arousing such general resentment that members of the societies were cowed into silence or into reversing their viewpoint.[38] In 1858 the legislature changed the name of Hancock County to Winston, honoring an Alabama governor instead of the old Revolutionary leader whom they now associated with abolitionism, and removed the name of the Missouri nationalist Thomas H. Benton from another county, renaming it for the states-righter John C. Calhoun.

Yet faced in 1860 by the prospect of actual war, many Alabamians entertained open doubt as to the wisdom of secession. Seventeen counties in northern Alabama sent "co-operationist" delegates to the convention of January 1861 to balk at "straight-out" secession and urge the more cautious course of concerted action with other Southern states. Thirty-three of these men refused to sign the ordinance of secession.[39] Robert Jemison of Tuscaloosa demanded to know what the firebrand secessionist William Lowndes Yancey planned to do with large numbers of citizens like himself who opposed leaving the Union: "Will he hang them by families, by neighborhoods, by towns, by counties, by Congressional districts?"[40]

Among the north Alabama farmers there was talk of seceding from Alabama and inviting mountain folk from Georgia and Tennessee to join them in forming a nonslave state by the Indian name of Nickajack.[41] Yancey was burned in effigy in Limestone County and it was rumored that, even after passage of the secession ordinance, the United States flag still flew over courthouses

38. Walter L. Fleming, *Civil War and Reconstruction in Alabama* (Cleveland: Arthur H. Clark Co., 1911), p. 10.

39. Carl N. Degler, *The Other South: Southern Dissenters in the Nineteenth Century* (New York: Harper and Row, Harper Torchbooks, 1974), pp. 170–171.

40. Thompson, *"Free State of Winston,"* pp. 20–24.

41. Elbert L. Watson, "The Story of the Nickajack," *Alabama Review* 20 (1967), 17–26.

in Athens and Huntsville. Divided in their sentiments, men of Elyton near the future site of Birmingham voted 675 to 574 against secession. [42]

Some older men of independent mind in the hills and wire-grass were not easily caught up in zeal for what they saw as a "rich man's war and a poor man's fight." Was it right that men who tilled their own fields should be asked to enlist for three years or for the uncertain duration of the war while owners of twenty slaves or more were initially exempt from service? James Bell, a barely literate citizen of Winston County, saw this as class privilege and bluntly advised his son Henry, who was wavering in favor of the Confederacy:

> I don't see what you nede to care for you hant got no slaves and all tha want is to git you pupt up and ga to fight for their infurnel negroes and after you do their fightin' you may kiss their hine parts for o tha care. [43]

Meeting at Looney's Tavern in Winston County, hill folk adopted a resolution commending C.C. Sheets, the twenty-two-year-old schoolteacher who had represented them at the secession convention, for holding firm to his promise to vote against leaving the Union "first, last and all of the time." [44] If a state could leave the Union, men at Looney's Tavern asked one another, could not a county secede from a state? This unanswered question earned their county a lasting sobriquet, "The Free State of Winston," and those who posed it were labelled "Tories."

But after the die was cast, most former co-operationists, the wealthy stagecoach operator Robert Jemison among them, joined the vast majority of Alabamians who placed loyalty to their state above attachment to the Union. Many made a pragmatic decision "if you can't beat 'em, join 'em." From Lawrence County a secessionist wrote Gov. A. B. Moore that ambitious men who hoped to become known in the state were

---

42. James H. Walker, Jr., *Roupes Valley* (Birmingham: privately printed, 1970), p. 37; Thompson *"Free State of Winston,"* p. 20.

43. Dodd, *Winston*, p. 79.

44. Dodd, *Winston*, p. 76.

not only becoming reconciled to secession but urging their followers to do likewise.[45]

Women played a considerable part in arousing enthusiasm for the Confederacy, those in the Black Belt stitching silken battle flags for their men, those in little hamlets like Westville in Dale County fashioning Confederate uniforms out of osnaburg, and girls of Winston County promising poor young men of the hills that service to the South could change their fortunes. P. D. Hall of Winston, an impressionable boy of sixteen in 1860, recalled that young women of slaveholding families who ordinarily would not associate with farm boys like himself, spoke openly to them of the honors of war and implied that those who fought for the Confederacy might expect to win their hands in marriage upon their return. Thus, Hall said, many "foolish boys" were tempted to enlist in the Confederate ranks.[46]

The first Confederate volunteers left Elyton under the impression that this war would be merely a skirmish, like the adventures of their fathers against Creeks and Seminoles, and that few lives would be lost. At Barnes Crossroads in Dale County, Jim Breer, captain of the home guards, promised volunteers: "This war won't amount to a hill of beans. . . . There will not be enough blood shed to stain this handkerchief in my hand . . . if you men go to war, you will have a pension for the rest of your lives." [47] But of 240 young men who left Westville in osnaburg uniforms made by their womenfolk, only 100 were to return.

Asked to shoot at "the flag of our fathers," loyalists in the hill country sought neutrality. But counties which lagged in filling their ranks of volunteers for the Confederacy were threatened with a draft from Montgomery. After the Confederacy passed a conscription act in 1862, neutralists hardened into Unionists, dissenters hid in mountain coves and caves rather than join the Rebel army, and many sneaked away to the natural rock bridge, a well-known Winston County landmark, to plan their escape into the Federal lines. Those who succeeded were

45. Degler, *The Other South*, p. 131.
46. Dodd, *Winston*, p. 271.
47. Watson, *Forgotten Trails*, p. 54.

formed into the First Alabama Union Cavalry, composed mostly of men from Winston, Walker, Fayette, Morgan, and Franklin counties, and would later march with Sherman through Georgia and the Carolinas. Others slipped into Union companies in Tennessee and Indiana. Their neighbors combed Winston's rockhouses and caves in search of them, imprisoning those whom they caught and harassing them to join the Confederate colors. Denman Turner of Easonville in St. Clair County, who was forced to join a Confederate unit, awaited his chance, waved a white handkerchief of surrender, and spent the rest of the war cooking for the Federals.[48]

Families of suspected Unionists found themselves blacklisted. Owners of gristmills would not grind their corn, ginners refused to process their cotton, and landowners evicted tenants. Storekeepers and blacksmiths would not serve them and they received little if any of the Confederacy's precious store of salt. Home guards and impressment agents plagued women, children, and the elderly left at home while their men hid out or went to war. Both Confederates and Yankees had assigned their least disciplined troops to the nonstrategic theater of northern Alabama and these cavalry units waged guerilla warfare through the hills, stealing cattle and horses, heedlessly burning stables, corncribs, and farm houses.[49]

The long conflict so brutalized men of both sides that legends of cruelty and torture still persist in the hill country. "Tories" waylaid and shot Dr. John Mangram, a Hamilton physician whom they suspected of informing on them. Confederate home guards reportedly tortured and hanged all six sons of William Hyde, a Winston Unionist. "Aunt Jenny" Brooks, whose husband was shot for harboring Unionists, became a folk heroine in Winston County because she reputedly made her children swear to avenge their father by killing every member of the raiding party, and eventually they carried out her wish. Confederates are said to have strung up one Unionist, placed splinters of "fat

48. Crow, *St. Clair County,* p. 65.

49. Hugh C. Bailey, "Disaffection in the Alabama Hill Country, 1861," *Civil War History* 4 (1958): 183–193; Fleming, *Civil War and Reconstruction,* p. 30.

pine" in his internal organs, and set him aflame. Unionists are reported to have hanged Ham Carpenter, the secession leader of Marion County, by his feet so that his head would be nearest the consuming fire. Confederates killed the probate judge of Winston County, Tom Pink Curtis, because they suspected that he was a Unionist. On his tombstone bitter relatives carved the words: "To the memory of T. P. Curtis. Was born November 27, 1829. Was killed by a Confederate raiding party January 19, 1864." [50]

Disaffection centered in the hill country but there was also evidence of desertion and a lack of zeal for the war in some south Alabama areas where slaves were few and cotton sparse. Henry, Dale, Coffee, and Covington counties reported desertions from Confederate units. The leading voice of dissent in this region was that of Alfred Holley of Andalusia, a prosperous farmer who served as justice of the peace, sheriff, and legislator for Covington County, strongly opposed secession, and voted against laws aimed at preparing the state for war. Defeated in 1861, Holley rallied enough antiwar sentiment in 1863 to win re-election for a fifth term and returned to the legislature to oppose every bill which he thought might prolong the war. On the sly Holley traded with Federal forces in Florida and helped Union prisoners escape to that state through the swamps of Covington. When Confederates learned of this activity, Holley was forced to seek political asylum with Union troops in Pensacola. His name was expunged as a "traitor" from the rolls of the Alabama House, and he moved to Milton, Florida, having sacrificed his holdings, his good name, and his career in Alabama politics for the cause of the Union.[51]

Historians continue to disagree as to the extent of Unionism in Alabama. Statistics show that 2,578 white Alabamians joined the Union army. One Winston County man alone, the tavern-keeper Bill Looney, is reputed to have spirited some 2,500 deserters to Union lines between 1862 and 1865. Hundreds of

50. Dodd, *Winston*, pp. 108, 258; Thompson, *"Free State of Winston,"* pp. 61–69, 92.

51. Jones, "Unionism and Disaffection in South Alabama," p. 132.

other Federal sympathizers, it is claimed, hid near home, formed bands of deserters and of those reluctant to be conscripted into Confederate service, acted as scouts for Union troops, and defended their mountain strongholds against Southern cavalry. Even Confederate Gen. Gideon J. Pillow conceded in 1862 that the Alabama mountains harbored 8,000 to 10,000 "Tories" and deserters. One historian of dissent in Alabama has stated that, had peace not come in 1865, the Peace Society which had flourished in Alabama since 1862 would have forced the state into a negotiated settlement. But an opposing viewpoint insists that disloyalty to the Confederacy was minimal in Alabama and confined largely to northern counties, notably Winston.[52]

Feelings about the war remained high in north Alabama after Appomattox as returning soldiers found their homes burned or looted, their friends and relatives killed. Animosities did not begin to fade away until after 1900. By then Denman Turner could joke openly about his defection to the Union, stating that he had merely gone over to the side which he thought was right in the first place. John S. Daniel of Cherokee County met up with a former neighbor, Joe Choate, who had fought for the Union when Daniel served the Confederacy. "At one time we were trying to kill each other," Daniel wrote his relatives, "but now we are friends." [53]

Yet as the Confederate legend bloomed with time, that of Alabama Unionists faded from memory and schoolroom history lessons. United Daughters of the Confederacy saw to it that almost every courthouse square in Alabama had its statue of Johnny Reb, rifle in hand, a symbol which helped convince later generations that the Southern cause went unquestioned in their state. Generations of schoolchildren were catechized on the exploits of native heroes and heroines like "Gallant" John Pel-

52. Bailey, "Disaffection in the Alabama Hill Country," p. 193; Dodd, *Winston*, p. 110; Durwood Long, "Unanimity and Disloyalty in Secessionist Alabama," *Civil War History* 11 (1965): 257–273.

53. Mrs. Frank Ross Stewart, *Cherokee County History, 1836–1956*, vol. 1 (Birmingham: Birmingham Printing Company, 1958), p. 91.

ham, the gifted artillery leader who gave his life for the Confederacy at twenty-four, and Emma Sansom, the country girl who guided Nathan Bedford Forrest to a river ford while Yankee bullets pierced her skirts. In history class they were afforded a chuckle over the mock-heroic tale that their aging ex-Confederate general, Joseph ("Fightin' Joc") Wheeler, serving the United States at San Juan Hill in 1898, mistook the Spaniards for his old foe and screeched: "Charge the damnyankees!" [54] Although such students were to serve in later wars, victories such as San Juan Hill, the Meuse-Argonne, and D-Day never stirred their emotions as did the bitter memory of defeat.

But as Alabamians reflect upon the two-hundredth anniversary of their nation's beginnings, it might not seem so heretical to recall this minority of the 1860s as loyalists to the United States rather than as traitors to the South. James Bell's declaration to his Confederate son that he "had jest as soon be cald a tory as to commit treason against the government that was sealed with the blood of my fathers" [55] might even be taken for patriotism.

Alabamians relish the scent of hickory in barbecue, a dash of pepper sauce on turnip greens, and a side order of tomfoolery with politics. Even in pioneer times the educated were familiar with the term used to denigrate politicians who play upon the emotions and prejudices of voters. Writing about Pickens County in 1856, a community historian described its people as peaceable and law-abiding "when let alone of demagogues." [56] Describing a congressman who represented northern Alabama for thirteen years, an observer of antebellum politics termed W. R. W. Cobb "the perfect type of demagogue." [57]

Cobb had first won notoriety with his bill to assure the

54. Malcolm C. McMillan, *The Land Called Alabama* (Austin, Texas: Steck-Vaughn Co., 1968), p. 260.

55. Dodd, *Winston*, p. 79.

56. Nelson F. Smith, *History of Pickens County, 1856* (reprinted in Elliott, comp., *Annals of Northwest Alabama*, 1); p. 91.

57. Willis Brewer, *Alabama: Her History, Resources, War Record and Public Men From 1540 to 1872* (Montgomery: Barrett and Brown, Printers, 1872), p. 286.

bankrupt of Alabama that, even if all their other possessions were sold for debt, they could keep a dozen cups and plates, a set of knives and forks, the coffee pot, two plows, some livestock, and the family portraits. He owed his election to Congress largely to this measure, which opponents derided as "rattling of tinware and crockery," and to his lusty renditions of a popular ditty, "The Homestead Bill," which began, "Uncle Sam is Rich Enough to Give Us All a Farm," and went on for many verses to promise furniture, housewares, mules, and other benefactions.[58] When Clement C. Clay, Jr., of Huntsville ran against Cobb in one election, Virginia Clay was outraged that her dignified and aristocratic husband should be defeated by a man who winked at members of the audience and chewed on onion and cornpone while he sang.[59]

But the fastidious Mrs. Clay represented only a wealthy minority in Cobb's mountainous district. The majority of voters were delighted when their congressman sang to them of the gifts they might expect from Washington and sensed that by his cornpone and winks Cobb was trying to evince a sincere concern for their welfare. Like most of his constituents, except the large slaveowners clustered around Huntsville and Decatur, Cobb opposed secession but, a slaveholder himself, he defended the concept that slaves were legal property. After delivering a lengthy and reluctant farewell to the House in 1861, Cobb was the last representative of a seceded state to leave Congress. When he refused to claim a seat in the Confederate Congress to which admirers had elected him, the rumor spread that Abraham Lincoln had offered to make Cobb military governor of Alabama. Angry Confederates voted unanimously to expel him from their Congress. Soon thereafter Cobb accidentally or intentionally shot himself to death.

Like Cobb, Felix Grundy McConnell of Talladega was a flamboyant member of Congress who favored homestead legis-

58. David Ritchey, "Williamson R.W. Cobb: Rattler of Tinware and Crockery for Peace," *Alabama Historical Quarterly* 36 (Summer 1974): 112–120.

59. Virginia Clay-Clopton, *A Belle of the Fifties* (New York: Doubleday, Page and Co., 1905), p. 21.

lation and whose career was to end in 1846 in apparent suicide. His home state admirers tolerated McConnell's openly acknowledged weakness for "the use of ardent spirits" but the fiery Alabamian proved something of a shock to staid Washingtonians. Caught up in the spirit of expansionism or perhaps alcoholism, McConnell once proposed the annexation of Ireland to the United States; on another occasion he astounded a sophisticated audience in the capital by interrupting a renowned violinist in the midst of an "exquisite performance" with the shouted command: "None of your highfalutin', but give us 'Hail Columbia,' and bear hard on the treble!" [60]

There were no antic politicians to equal McConnell and Cobb until the early decades of the twentieth century when J. Thomas Heflin, an imposing figure when attired for the stump in his white frock coat and flowing tie, enthralled voters with oratorical cadences like this: "Cotton is a child of the sun. It is kissed by the silvery beams of a southern moon and bathed in the crystal dewdrops that fall in the silent watches of the night." [61] But genial "Cotton Tom" could also make an audience shudder at the thought of Popish plots or roar at racist jokes about "a nigger and an' ole mule" and homespun stories like the one about the rube who didn't believe that sounds would carry over the newfangled contraption called a telephone. Finally persuaded to listen for the voice of his wife, the country fellow put the receiver to his ear just as lightning crackled and thunder clapped, whereupon (declared Heflin) he let out a yell: "That's her all right! That shore is my ole woman!" Clarence Cason, a professor of English, admired such ability to handle the language and insisted that "it was worth travelling a hundred miles over bad roads to hear Tom Heflin speak." [62] Many Alabamians agreed, dispatching Heflin to Congress for three decades.

Heflin might have stayed in the Senate until his dying day had

60. Quoted in Leah Rawls Atkins, "Southern Congressmen and the Homestead Bill," (Ph.D. diss., Auburn University, 1974), pp. 97–98.

61. Ralph M. Tanner, "Senator Tom Heflin as Storyteller," *Alabama Review* 15 (1963): 54–60.

62. Cason, *90° in the Shade,* pp. 78–88.

it not been for the national hubbub over "rum, Romanism, and rebellion." Although a lifelong Democrat, "Cotton Tom" was a leader of the revolt in Alabama against his party's 1928 presidential nominee, Alfred E. Smith. When Democrats chose a wet, Catholic candidate whose accent over the "rad-dio" grated harshly on southern ears, Heflin threatened to bolt, confiding to the voters that he could eat crow but not "buzzard with Tammany sauce." [63] To punish such apostasy, Democrats in 1930 barred Heflin from seeking re-election on their ticket. Forced to run as an independent, Heflin was defeated by John H. Bankhead, Jr. Although he contested the election, he was eventually forced to yield his seat to Bankhead and live out his remaining years in political exile. During his thirty years in public office, Heflin had often sought to help cotton farmers and had associated himself during the 1920s with the progressive "farm bloc" in Congress. But when it came to individual legislative achievement he could boast only that he had authored the bill establishing Mother's Day. [64]

During the 1920s loiterers around courthouse squares favored other politicians with names that rolled majestically on the tongue like Lycurgus Breckenridge Musgrove and Hugo La-Fayette Black. "Breck" Musgrove had gotten his fancy name because his grandfather, an early judge in Jasper, had been a scholar of the classics. Although "Breck" owned enough property in coal mines, banks, and the rural press to qualify as a rich man, he appealed for votes by claiming to drink nothing stronger than persimmon beer, relating how his father lost a leg fighting for the Confederacy, and promising to throw out "fossiliferous old asses of reaction" like Sen. Oscar W. Underwood. [65]

Musgrove came within an ace of unseating the conservative and prominent Underwood in 1920. Alarmed at his political prospects, the elderly senator retired at the end of his term,

63. Hamilton, *Hugo Black,* p. 154.

64. Ralph M. Tanner, "James Thomas Heflin: United States Senator, 1920–1931" (Ph.D. diss. University of Alabama, 1967) is a study of Heflin's career.

65. Hamilton, *Hugo Black,* pp. 73–75.

thereby setting off a political free-for-all. Hugo Black was the youngest and least-known candidate in this 1926 race but he was shrewdly attuned to the hopes and frustrations of the plain folk among whom he had spent his youth. Having no wealthy backers nor ties with the traditional oligarchy, Black had joined the Ku Klux Klan. During the campaign he enjoyed the Klan's powerful support even though he had placed a letter of resignation in its secret files so he would be free to assure Jews, Catholics, and others that he was not a member.

Black wooed rural folk with promises of cheap fertilizer, a veterans' bonus, better roads, and bans on immigrants; pleaded with newly enfranchised mothers to strike down the idea that "only the rich and powerful sons of the great can serve their state"; assured the pious that he had never tasted whiskey, and amused audiences with his jingle: "There's one little saloon that every man can close, and that is the one which is under his nose." [66] While the two most prominent candidates engaged one another in joint debate, the future Supreme Court justice hired a black driver and mule-drawn dray to parade around town with a sign which read: "Bankhead Say Kilby Won't Do. Kilby Say Bankhead Won't Do. Both are Right. Vote for Hugo Black!" [67] Enough voters complied to send Hugo Black to the United States Senate and set him upon the road to the court.

Another son of Clay County, Henry J. Carwile, tried to win the governorship during the Second World War with a red, white, and blue Model T and a platform that was hard to oppose: "Rescue the perishing and care for the dying." [68] But Carwile was out-politicked by James E. Folsom, a native of the wiregrass transplanted to Cullman County, who resembled the comic strip hero Lil' Abner in giant stature, unruly black hair, and rustic good looks. Folsom's own hero was Andrew Jackson but "Big Jim" knew that twentieth-century Jacksonians

---

66. Hamilton, *Hugo Black*, p. 131.
67. Hamilton, *Hugo Black*, p. 128.
68. William D. Barnard, "The Old Order Changes: Graves, Sparks, Folsom, and the Gubernatorial Election of 1942," *Alabama Review* 28 (1976): 172–173.

could not be enticed to come pouring out of the "branch heads" merely to express their democratic aspirations at the polls. "Y'all come!" Folsom exhorted, offering to entertain them with his string band, "The Strawberry Pickers," and promising to kiss the women and pave the dusty roads. While his supporters passed the "suds bucket" for donation, "Kissin' Jim" excoriated the "Big Mules" of Alabama industry and agriculture and demanded more state services, repeal of the poll tax, reapportionment, and constitutional reform. This platform and his rustic charisma won Folsom two terms in the governor's chair.[69]

During the Great Depression and Second World War, many rural folk moved to Mobile and Birmingham but had not become too citified to appreciate a politician who could coin a homely slogan or write a bit of doggerel with which they could identify. Voters of the Mobile district sending Frank Boykin to represent them in Congress for fourteen terms was due in no small measure to his frequent incantation, "Everything's Made for Love!" Mobilians found Boykin an engaging fellow even after he was convicted in United States District Court on eight counts of conspiracy to defraud his country by violating conflict of interest laws, fined $40,000, and put on six-months' probation. Friends in Congress persuaded President Lyndon Johnson to grant the eighty-year-old ex-congressman a pardon, whereupon Boykin airily dismissed the whole affair as "just like a traffic violation." [70]

Boykin's congressional colleague from Birmingham was Luther Patrick, a bucolic versifier who represented that district for four terms. Patrick, although a friend to the laboring man, wrote no major legislation but he did compose a widelyread poem entitled "A-Sleepin' at the Foot of the Bed." This ode, a portion of which follows, provided many readers with a simple excuse for their lack of worldly achievement:

69. William D. Barnard, *Dixiecrats and Democrats, Alabama Politics, 1942–1950* (University, Ala.: University of Alabama Press, 1974) treats Folsom's early political career.

70. *Birmingham Post-Herald*, December 21, 1965.

Did you ever sleep at the foot of the bed when the weather wuz
  whizzin' cold,
When the wind was whistlin' around the house and the moon
  wuz yaller as gold,
You give your good warm mattress up to Aunt Lizzie and Uncle
  Fred. . . .
I've done it over and over again in this land of the brave and the
  free
And in this all fired battle of life, it's left its mark on me
For I'm always a-strugglin' around at the foot instead of forgin'
  ahead
And I don't think it's caused from a doggone thing but
  A-SLEEPIN' AT THE FOOT OF THE BED.[71]

Eugene "Bull" Connor, the son of a railroad dispatcher in
Selma, was among those south Alabamians who sought to improve their lot by moving to Birmingham. Connor attracted
favor as a baseball announcer with a special flare for drawling
the phrase, "He's OWwww-you-IT!" Elected as Birmingham's
public safety commissioner, Connor served twenty years,
achieving international notoriety in 1963 for his use of police
dogs and fire hoses upon young black civil rights demonstrators.
Alarmed at their city's harsh image, Birmingham citizens rejected Connor in the next election but Alabama's rural voters
applauded "ole Bull " and elevated him to the office of state
public service commissioner.

All this rattling of tinware, waving the "bloody shirt" of
Civil War or the white ribbon of Prohibition, joking about "ole
niggers," fabricating Catholic plots, and contriving simplistic
slogans and poems, which has vivified Alabama politics for
more than a century, was not merely a show calculated to lure
plain folk to the voting booths. Shrewd politicians sensed the
deep frustration of the white majority who felt ill used by those
whom their champions called "fossiliferous old asses of reac-

---

71. "A-Sleepin' at the Foot of the Bed," words by Luther Patrick. © Copyright
1949 by Acuff-Rose Publications, Inc., 2510 Franklin Rd., Nashville 4, Tennessee.
Used with permission.

tion," "rich and powerful sons of the great," and "Big Mules." Such voters hoped to put someone in office who actually would support laws to console them in case of bankruptcy, assure higher prices for their crops and lower prices for fertilizer, improve the roads, educate their children, and protect them from the competition of convicts, immigrants, and blacks who worked even more cheaply than they.

In the 1880s and 1890s bitter farmers found words of their own to voice dissatisfaction. Writing to county newspapers, they griped that landlords figured "3 times 3 are nine and the crop's all mine" and complained that they had to fish at night to supplement their diet of "poke sallet" and pepper grass. One feared that his children "were doomed to grow up in ignorance to become 'hewers of wood and drawers of water' for a more fortunate few." Another angry correspondent railed that people like himself had been imposed upon "ever since old father Adam was farming on the Uphrates [*sic*] river." [72]

Such farmers found a handy target for their grievances in the local "furnishing merchants" who advanced them seed, coffee, clothes, or other needs at high prices and extravagant rates of interest, taking a lien on their cotton or a mortgage on their land and personal belongings as security. When time came to settle up, most farmers had little to show for a year of hard toil or, like an increasing number of onetime landowners, were forced to forfeit their land and sink into sharecropping and tenantry. Merchants, for their part, felt that they took a precarious risk by advancing goods to fifty or a hundred families. One store owner in Greenville advertised: "You made the mortgage, and you ate up and wore out the goods, and you never paid for them. Now settle and stop this eternal slandering and whining around and pay up and give satisfaction and be a man." [73]

Rather than sharecrop, thousands of whites who lost their land went to work during the 1890s in cotton mills where they

72. William Warren Rogers, *The One-Gallused Rebellion: Agrarianism in Alabama, 1865–1896* (Baton Rouge: Louisiana State University Press, 1970), pp. 18, 148, 236.

73. Margaret Pace Farmer, "Furnishing Merchants and Sharecroppers in Pike County, Alabama," *Alabama Review* 23 (1970): 143–151.

were sequestered from the economic competition of blacks and provided with housing, churches, schools, and stores by paternalistic employers who fiercely and successfully contested all efforts to unionize them. By 1900 almost 9,000 men, women, and children were employed in Alabama mills at wages so low that the whole family had to work as they had on the farm.[74]

In 1902 Edgar Gardner Murphy, a crusading Episcopal rector in Montgomery, published a series of pamphlets showing photographs of mill children in Alabama, including that of a six-year-old boy who worked twelve hours at a machine for a total of fifteen cents a day, and that of three barefoot boys, seven to nine years of age, who labored six days a week from 5:20 A.M. to 6:30 P.M. except during rush periods when they worked until 10:00 P.M.[75] An Alabama law of 1887, limiting a child's working day to eight hours, had been repealed in 1895 upon the demand of a Massachusetts company which was constructing a large mill in the state. In organizing the Alabama Child Labor Committee, Murphy achieved some reform by persuading the Alabama legislature of 1907 to pass a law setting the minimum age of child workers at twelve, limiting their work week to sixty hours, and forbidding those under sixteen to work the all-night shift.

In rebellion over their lot, plain whites surged against the barricades of economic and political power repeatedly in the late nineteenth century. Although met by implacable hostility farmers and tenants struggled to make themselves heard, first through the Grange and later in the more radical organizations of the Farmers' Alliance and Agricultural Wheel. The Grange, originally a social and educational society, enlarged its program to advocate that "furnishing merchants" be replaced by co-operative stores to serve the needs of farmers, that tenants be paid wages rather than a share of the crop, and that legislative seats be filled by more farmers and by fewer lawyers, merchants, and

74. Moore, *History of Alabama*, p. 532.
75. Hugh C. Bailey, *Edgar Gardner Murphy: Gentle Progressive* (Coral Gables, Fla.: University of Miami Press, 1968), pp. 83–106.

railroad men. By 1877 almost 15,000 Alabama farmers had joined the Grange.[76]

When the Grange faded away, the turbulent Wheel took up the farmers' cause, entering Alabama in the Tennessee valley and attracting some 75,000 members by 1889 through appeals for co-op factories as well as co-op stores and by outcries against the jute bagging trust and the high rates of the Louisville and Nashville Railroad. The Wheel in turn was absorbed into the mushrooming Farmers' Alliance, which spread southward from the Tennessee valley to the piney woods and wiregrass until in 1889 it could boast 125,000 members in 3,000 lodges plus 50,000 in the separate but like-minded Colored Farmers' Alliance. The Alliance inspired a rash of co-op stores, warehouses, fertilizer and cottonseed oil plants, hotels, and even a state cotton exchange, the largest business undertaking launched by a farm group in Alabama. But price wars, mismanagement, and economic depression doomed these enterprises. In the early 1890s the Alliance followed the Grange and Wheel into oblivion.

Farm unrest culminated in revolt from the "white man's party" which had been regarded as sacrosanct ever since its leaders won the nickname of "Bourbons" for redeeming Alabama from Reconstruction. Democrats, with good reason, feared that the "one-gallused rebellion" might unite whites with blacks and ally disaffected farmers with the restive laborers of Birmingham who had joined first the Knights of Labor and later the United Mine Workers of Alabama in hope of winning higher wages. When coal miners struck in 1894, the governor dispatched state militia to protect "blacklegs" imported to replace them. Their employers leased state convicts at $108 a year per man to dig the coal in their stead.

The political upheaval, variously called the Peoples' party, Populism, and Jeffersonian Democracy, burgeoned during the hard times of the early 1890s. Its Alabama leader, Reuben Kolb, a renegade from the planter class, made strenuous cam-

76. Rogers, *One-Gallused Rebellion*, pp. 63–78.

paigns for the governorship in 1892 and 1894 only to be "counted out" when Black Belt counties returned highly suspect majorities for the regular Democratic candidate. Kolb cried fraud, claiming that these boxes had been stuffed with the ballots of intimidated blacks, dead men, and faithful hounds. Most historians agreed that Kolb would have won in an honest count.[77]

Blacks were a central issue in these campaigns. When Populists attempted to capture the black vote in 1892, Democrats branded them traitors to the white South. But black votes, the balance of power, were used and misused by Democrats to maintain white supremacy. To remove the threat of future revolts and the possibility of an interracial coalition of the underdogs, Democrats rewrote the franchise provisions of the Alabama constitution in 1901, greatly reducing the number of poor white voters and virtually excluding blacks from the polls.[78]

During the 1920s, however, spiritual descendants of Populists welded an irresistible coalition of drys, fundamentalists, war veterans, and Ku Klux Klansmen and actually captured the governorship. They not only seated their champion Bibb Graves in the governor's chair but dispatched Hugo Black to the United States Senate, where colleagues regarded him disdainfully at first as a hillbilly lawyer. But the Klan and its cohorts held political control only briefly. By 1930, disgraced by excesses of violence, Knights of the Invisible Empire had fallen from power in Alabama, leaving Bibb Graves and Hugo Black to scramble for other means of retaining their political offices.[79]

It was the federal government during Franklin Roosevelt's New Deal which finally set a minimum wage, shortened the

---

77. Robert David Ward and William Warren Rogers, *Labor Revolt in Alabama: The Great Strike of 1894* (University, Ala.: University of Alabama Press, 1965), pp. 20–34.

78. The Constitutional Convention of 1901 is described at length in Francis Sheldon Hackney, *Populism to Progressivism in Alabama* (Princeton: Princeton University Press, 1969) and Malcolm C. McMillan, *Constitutional Development in Alabama, 1798–1901: A Study in Politics, the Negro, and Sectionalism,* vol. 37, James Sprunt Studies in History and Political Science (Chapel Hill: University of North Carolina Press, 1955).

79. Hamilton, *Hugo Black,* pp. 119–170; William E. Gilbert, "Bibb Graves as a Progressive, 1927–1930," *Alabama Review* 10 (1957): 15–30.

work week, took children out of cotton mills, and guaranteed the right to join a union. The Tennessee Valley Authority coaxed many hill people out of their coves and into the mainstream by offering them the alternative of working for wages in new industries. Those who clung to the land were taught to redeem their wasted soil. TVA and the Rural Electrification Administration stretched the first power lines to remote areas where people in the 1930s still cooked and heated by wood fires, boiled their clothes in iron pots, pressed with heavy "sad irons," kept milk and butter in wells, and pushed back the darkness with candles and kerosene lamps. Before electric lines reached them, a family which "lost its fire" sent a child to the neighbors for a hot coal or resorted to the luxury of using a sulphur match. Preparing to strike a match, a father in St. Clair County summoned all his children to witness the big event. When electricity finally reached her, a rural housewife expressed her heartfelt gratitude: "Wonder of all wonders, this delivery from the prison of isolation and darkness and drudgery." [80]

The federal government also subsidized rural schools and hospitals, simplified voting procedures, and ordered that Alabama be redistricted to give more political representation to populous, urbanized areas. But Washington has gotten little thanks for conferring such economic and political benefactions on Alabama. Most white citizens, still smarting at the recollection of how the federal government forced them to concede civil rights to blacks, tend today to cuss "the feds" for inflicting high taxes and prices on working folk, burdening them with bureaucracy, and failing to protect them from crime.

Insofar as political affairs inside their own state are concerned, descendants of the spirited Alliance and Populists are freed from the frustration under which their ancestors chafed. Amid the uproar which followed *Brown* v. *Board of Education of Topeka* in 1954, their man Jim Folsom became a political casualty of his moderate racial views, of the powerful, conservative opposition which he aroused, and of his own weakness for

80. Elliott, *Annals of Northwest Alabama*, 1, p. 207.

liquor. However, their more recent hero George Wallace, with the help of his first wife, the late Lurleen Wallace, was firmly in the saddle of Alabama politics for more than a decade.

Thousands who might be described still as poor whites remain mired in poverty and ignorance on Alabama's byways. But numerous descendants of sturdy farmers have become skilled artisans, attained a passable degree of comfort (thanks largely to federal wage scales and unionization), live in brick bungalows or split-level houses, and enjoy color television, motorcycles, powerboats, and a weekend cottage on the lake. Others have risen even higher in the middle-class hierarchy through the ministry, education, or business. Grandsons of Populists have become prosperous lawyers or doctors, with swimming pools in their backyards; daughters of farmers and Klansmen belong to country clubs and devote their mornings to golf.

When presidential election time comes round, the majority of these white Alabamians have been prone to follow wherever George Wallace led them. However, the most affluent can be seen in Republican voting lines. In either case they aim their political slings and arrows almost entirely in the direction of Washington, seldom mounting any concerted campaigns against those Alabamians who are the "Bourbons" and "Big Mules" of today. To rant against the system as did their feisty ancestors is out of fashion and would likely be viewed with suspicion as yet another Communist plot.

Politics like farming had a "laying-by time" when no orators, poets, singers, or sloganeers mounted the stump to lend a carnival air to the backwoods. For diversion, pioneers depended on rituals like sorghum making, hog killing, hunting, and fishing. In hope of garnering news and gossip of the outside world, they offered hospitality to travellers such as churn peddlers, tanners, or that most prestigious of all visitors, the circuit preacher or revivalist whose status merited chicken for dinner and ham at breakfast.

Educated travellers from faraway parts rarely sought shelter in a ordinary farm home. Yet Frederick Law Olmsted, a journalist and gentleman farmer from New York who toured the antebellum South, proved to be inquisitive about agrarians of all levels. Passing through northern Alabama in 1853, Olmsted found the farm people whom he visited to be kindly, hospitable, and as curious about him as he about them. He noted that these white men and women worked in the fields themselves, attended their thin soil diligently yet raised meager crops. "They are very ignorant," he concluded compassionately. "The agriculture is wretched and the work hard." [81]

Other travellers passed through the Alabama highlands each fall herding vast numbers of hogs and mules to Tuscaloosa for shipment down the Warrior and Tombigbee to market. These Tennessee drovers sent an advance courier to advertise their willingness to barter, arrived with a flurry of hunting horns and trumpet calls, and announced in a lusty Elizabethan chant that they had interests beyond mere trading:

> Hog drovers, hog drovers, hog drovers we are,
> Come courting your daughters so lovely and fair. [82]

Sorghum makers too came in the fall, bringing the mill and huge pan necessary to reduce the cane crop to syrup. If abundantly fed, these men worked day and night until an entire crop had been ground. Pine knot torches illuminated the scene, mules plodded a ceaseless merry-go-round to pull the lever which operated the mill, and neighbors, attracted by the sound of crackling cane and the aroma of steaming syrup, gathered to swap tall tales and share in the convivial atmosphere. Hog killing was another harbinger of winter, a gory but essential ritual by which hogs were converted to ham, bacon, chops, sausage, chitlings, spareribs, souse, and lard, even their bladders inflated and given to children as balloons. [83]

Hunters and fishermen found game so bounteous that modern sportsmen reading their accounts might well shed a tear. Settlers

81. Olmsted, *Journey in the Back Country*, pp. 205–220.
82. Walker, *Roupes Valley*, pp. 27–28.
83. Many local historians describe the rites of hog killing but none more vividly than Viola Goode Liddell, *With a Southern Accent* (Norman: University of Oklahoma Press, 1948), pp. 150–153.

along the Warrior and Cahaba recorded that those streams were so limpid that they could spot a trout in ten feet of water. Flocks of bronze turkeys frequented the hill country. One St. Clair County hunter returned from a day's outing in 1874 with nine of these wild birds across his shoulder. Pigeon, quail, dove, duck, geese, squirrel, opossum, and coon were plenteous; deer and bears roamed the river banks. Many huntsmen bartered their game for household articles while men of more daring nature took their price in cash to bet against the gamblers of Frog Valley race track near Tuscaloosa.

Yet the central figure of this arcadian scene who attended his crop so industriously, welcomed a stranger warmly, worshipped God fervently, and for the most part displayed good humor, also indulged in pursuits which betrayed a darker side of his nature. Following ancestral practices which dated back to Elizabethan times, he wrenched the greased neck off a struggling gander for sport, gouged his opponent's eye from its socket to win a brawl, and hanged his neighbor by a noose to satisfy his concept of justice.

Scholars have long puzzled over the causes of the notorious violence of southern white folk, believing it an oversimplification to blame such behavior solely upon racial antagonism. In antebellum Alabama, white men frequently wreaked mayhem upon one another in bloody brawling or lynched fellow whites whom they judged transgressors. Feuds in the Alabama highlands were fewer than in the Kentucky and Tennessee mountains. Duels were less frequent than among lowland planters. These plain folk settled their scores in single-handed combat with knife, fist, or gun. If sufficiently goaded by passion, they set their victim atop a primitive cart, tied a rope from a tree limb around his neck, signalled the mules to "git up!" and watched impassively as the noose did its work. On the edges of the crowd, Indians gaped at this strange custom of those who proclaimed themselves civilized.

Did this violence of white against white stem from the reckless individualism of the Scotch-Irish? From a need to act out fantasies of manhood and behave with the braggadocio of heroes? Could it be attributed to the frontier tendency toward summary justice or to poverty, backwardness, rurality, child-beating, a profusion of guns, or the very climate itself? Is it a bastard offspring of religious fundamentalism? Scholars agree as to the existence of extraordinary violence in the South yet are at a loss to define its precise cause or to say whether it results from a single factor alone. Mulling over this enigma, one historian even resorted to quoting the explanation supposedly given to a self-righteous Yankee critic by a laconic southerner who reckoned that there were just more folks in the South who needed killing.[84]

Frederick Olmsted, a moderate who favored gradual emancipation over abrupt abolition, was one of those northerners who was curious as to how slaveowning had affected the southern psyche. He found the racism of Alabama farm folk somewhat tempered by their first-hand knowledge of how gruelling it was to plow, hoe, and weed under the southern sun. One poor white told Olmsted: "I'd ruther be dead than to be a nigger on one of those big plantations." In another household Olmsted overheard this comment upon a white laborer who had been dismissed for rapping fellow black workers with a hoe handle: "He was a heap meaner n' niggers. I reckon niggers would come somewhere between white folks and such as he." Olmsted observed that blacks appeared to have more individual freedom in north Alabama than in the lowlands. But these white farmers, fearful of the effects of emancipation upon their own lives, could envision no solution save the continuance of slavery. Almost universally they told Olmsted: "It wouldn't never do to free 'em and leave 'em here." [85]

This viewpoint would prove tragically prophetic. After war produced the emancipation which they dreaded, whites turned from brawling, gander pulling, and lynching one another to concentrate their hostilities upon those whom they perceived as new threats. Seeping south from its birthplace in Tennessee, the Ku

---

84. Sheldon Hackney, "Southern Violence," *American Historical Review* 74 (1969): 906–926. See also John Sheldon Reed, "To Live—and Die—in Dixie: A Contribution to the Study of Southern Violence," *Political Science Quarterly* 86 (1971): 429–443.
85. Olmsted, *Journey in the Back Country,* pp. 202–220.

Klux Klan made its debut in northern Alabama in 1867 and set out to terrorize white Republicans, former Unionists, northern missionaries, and the freedmen. By garbing themselves as vigilantes, plain folk were not merely following their old Confederate leaders in an effort to reinstate home rule and white supremacy. Although exact motives are impossible to ascertain, one historian has surmised that many of the rank-and-file night riders found the Klan not just a means of "keepin' a nigger in his place," (well below their own) but another form of violent sport, an opportunity to rob, protect their illicit distilleries, or wreak personal vengeance upon their enemies under the guise of honor.[86]

Whatever their impetus, sheeted men with guns, whips, and horses rampaged almost at will through the northern counties. Bands of 300 Klansmen were seen in Huntsville. The judicial process in Blount County was reported so tightly controlled by the Klan that no grand jury would indict, no trial jury convict. Morgan and Fayette counties were scenes of guerilla warfare between the Klan and native white Unionists called Mossybacks. Ryland Randolph, a hotheaded editor with a talent for appealing to the basest instincts of his readers, was the power behind the Klan in Tuscaloosa County. As an aftermath of racial disturbances in Calhoun County in 1870, Klansmen hanged four black youths and a white male schoolteacher who had come from Canada to instruct the former slaves. This mass lynching aroused a national furor. Cross Plains, the community in which it took place, later changed its name to Piedmont.[87]

"Terrorism and anarchy reins [sic] in this county," an alarmed Republican in Lauderdale complained to Gov. William H. Smith. Although bombarded with appeals, Smith refrained from imposing martial law, perhaps in fear of turning northern Alabama into a virtual battleground between a predominantly white militia and the white legions of the Klan. By 1871 the tide

---

86. Ray Granade, "Violence: An Instrument of Policy in Reconstruction Alabama," *Alabama Historical Quarterly* 86 (1971): 181–201.

87. Allen W. Trelease, *White Terror: The Ku Klux Klan Conspiracy and Southern Reconstruction* (New York: Harper and Row, 1971), pp. 81–87, 265–270.

of terrorism began to recede as Democrats made political gains, federal prosecutors became more zealous, and satiated Alabamians demanded an end to the violence.[88]

Yet sporadically over the next hundred years plain whites engaged in new sprees of violence, usually at tragic cost to blacks. Numerous lynchings were an offshoot of the economic and political tensions of the 1890s. The Klan, resurrected during the First World War, became not only the most powerful political force in Alabama during the 1920s but a scourge of Catholics, Jews, immigrants from southern and eastern Europe, Orientals, blacks, alcoholic tipplers, divorced persons, and any others branded by its membership as sinners or undesirables. Birmingham Klansmen flogged their city's health officer whom they accused of "Kaiser-like acts." Masked men in Oneonta whipped a mildly intoxicated young white man with an automobile fan belt until his back was covered by welts and his legs blue with blood clots. Twenty persons were flogged, some fatally, in Crenshaw County where, declared the state attorney general, a virtual reign of terror existed. As in the 1870s the Klan overreached itself, aroused a public backlash, lost membership, and fell from power.

Carl Carmer, observing Alabama in the 1920s, concluded that this was "a land of quick reactions, of sudden and stunning violence." When he explored racial attitudes, he was told by some whites in the hills that they were simply unaccustomed to seeing black faces: "Feller round here tol' me he got to votin' age 'fore he ever seen one." [89] Descendants of the German founders of Cullman are reputed to have posted the warning: "Nigger, don't let the sun set on you in this town!" [90]

Early in the 1930s crowds of menacing whites, gathering outside the courthouses of Scottsboro and Decatur, made it unmistakably clear to judges and jurors that they wanted quick conviction of the nine black "Scottsboro boys" accused of raping two

88. Trelease, *White Terror,* pp. 261–265.

89. Carl Carmer, *Stars Fell on Alabama,* pp. 16–17, 69.

90. Elliott, *Annals of Northwest Alabama,* 3 (Tuscaloosa: privately printed, 1965), pp. 26–27.

white women aboard a freight train.[91] One ninety-three-year-old man in Blount County made a simple but frank admission of the racial prejudice of his people. "We are Scotch-Irish," said Forrest Lee Culbreath. "We do not believe in mixing with the Negro." [92]

During the turbulent civil rights demonstration of the 1960s many white Alabamians again reacted violently when blacks demanded the right to vote, to ride in any seat on the bus, to eat at the same lunch counters, use the same rest rooms, and attend the same schools as whites. Plain folk sensed that it was *they*, not the most prosperous whites, who were to ride buses, live in neighborhoods, and compete for jobs with blacks; *their* children who were to be seated alongside black children in schools.

But the sight of white demonstrators from the North goaded them to even greater fury. Here came another wave of outsiders retracing the steps of all those old abolitionists, Yankee soldiers, school teachers, missionaries, and federal judges who had meddled in the affairs of their state. Their bitter resentment of those whom they called "white niggers" also had an undertone of jealousy. By their taunts and threats, the poorest white element was expressing not only a deeply-ingrained racism but fear, drummed into them for generations, that their precarious station would be diminished if the day of racial justice should ever dawn. Yet the nation observed them on television with distaste, perceived their forebodings and ignorance only as brutality, and failed to recognize that here were other oppressed people to whose rescue no avengers from afar had ever flown.

The fact that Alabama, although fancying its plantation antecedents, is more literally an offspring of the rough American West will bear repeating. Enchanted for a century by the portrait of a coquettish Southern Belle, its citizens may be reluctant to claim a linsey-woolsey ancestor with a dip of snuff tucked under her lip. But pause before a tintype of this solemn, unadorned

---

91. Dan T. Carter, *Scottsboro: A Tragedy of the American South* (Baton Rouge: Louisiana State University Press 1969) is the definitive work on this famous case.

92. Elliott, *Annals of Northwest Alabama*, 1: 172.

countenance to reflect upon the stubborn persistence of her nine-teenth-century mores in a society ever modernizing, urbanizing, and homogenizing. Her legacy, though homespun, is tenacious.

To begin with an obvious example, consider the abiding affection for pioneer foods prepared as nearly as possible in her iron pot tradition. Although Alabamians have succumbed to the neon lure of "fast foods," they remain devoted to slow cookery, continuing to boil, simmer, and stew their turnip greens, collards, and "poke sallet" with a ham bone or chunk of "fatback" for flavor. No culinary skill is more highly regarded than the knack of producing light, crisp cornbread or "pone" from a heavy mold or skillet. Despite Yankee sneers, Alabamians still relish their breakfast "grits," a delicacy savored by their forebears who made a dessert from the "grits" which remained after corn had been beaten with wooden pestles and sifted through coarse sieves. Although persimmon wine is rare today, chestnuts have all but disappeared, and watercress does not thrive in polluted streams, there is still sassafras root to purify the blood in springtime, plenty of catfish to fry in deep fat, and ample pork to satisfy an apparently insatiable taste for barbecue smeared with hot sauce.

The disappearance of the horse-and-buggy doctor, his black bag filled with quinine, alum, castor oil, and calomel, has left many an Alabama community bereft of modern medical services. But these isolated people, if lacking a doctor, can still fall back upon the folk remedies of their self-reliant and ingenious ancestors, brewing a cup of catnip tea for the baby with colic, rubbing camphor on the chest of one suffering from a cold, applying stump water to warts, and, if bitten by a rabid dog, rushing to fetch that family treasure, the "madstone" of a deer, to draw off the poison.

Rural music also has its enduring appeal. Carl Carmer, observing a fiddling contest in the 1920s when destitute farm folk could afford little other diversion, fancied that the audience, even though a century removed from pioneer origins, heard creaking axles, cries of wild beasts, and echoes of hard work when a fiddler tucked his instrument under his chin and began to play "Old Cow Died in the Forks of the Branch," "Wolves A-

Howlin'," "Cotton Choppin' Dick," "Rum Has Made a Fool Out 'a Me," "Whole Hog or None," "Mountaintop Cabin," "Fire in the Mountains," and "Rocky Hollow Hard Times." At one time such contests almost disappeared in the face of competition from television, football, and auto racing but there has recently been a revival of interest in fiddling. Spiritual descendants of the old-time fiddlers cut discs of blue grass and country music in Sheffield and Muscle Shoals today and their plaintive sounds virtually monopolize Alabama radio waves. At harvest time each year the Municipal Auditorium in Birmingham is filled for several evenings by the children and grandchildren of those who once gathered in the churchyard for all-day sings, propelled to the city now by some inner yearning to hear and voice the same old hymns.

Language too has its lingering flavor of the frontier. Scholars say that it has been shaped by old English expressions, the desire of frontiersmen to show friendliness, the debilitating climate, the association with blacks, a lack of schooling, and custom itself. Plenty of Alabamians still pronounce their *e*'s like *i* ("in gin'ral"), use "carry" for "take" ("I'm carryin' my mother to the store"), speak of their midday meal as dinner and of afternoon as evening, and use double words for emphasis (widow-woman, boss-man, tooth-dentist). Some deep in the hills even retain a biblical poesy in their speech. "We don't have much but what we have we give unto thee," a mountain man told Carl Carmer.[93]

Pioneer children respected Pa for his knowledge of crops and animals and his abilities at shooting, fiddling, or fist fighting. Despite her subordinate role in frontier society, her children looked up to Ma for her skill in cooking, gardening, crafts, and square dancing. In an era when many parents complain that their children have lost all esteem for them, Alabama youth, even those of affluent middle-class background, continue to address parents, teachers, and other elders with at least the outward forms of respect, "yes" being customarily followed by "sir," and "no" softened by the addition of "ma'am." Typical

93. Carmer, *Stars Fell on Alabama*, p. 66.

parents, strongly fortified by community and church, have retained the loyalty of their children to a greater degree than have their counterparts in other regions. Youthful rebellion has been held to a minimum but at considerable cost to the venturesomeness, openmindedness, and broad education of the newer generation.

Many white adults still say "sir" and "ma'am" to those whom they sense to be of a higher social order. They do not mean to indicate class antagonism and there is no surliness in this manner of address. It is verbal evidence that such white Alabamians have a sense of class distinctions although they seldom harbor deep or lasting hostility toward their more fortunate fellows. More than a century ago Frederick Olmsted was struck by the kindly nature of Alabama plain folk. Reuben Davis, a nineteenth-century political leader in Winston County, marvelled that his neighbors, despite heavy toll and much privation, remained eminently sociable and hospitable. Milton Fies, transplanted from the East to become the foremost developer of Alabama coal mines, was one of many industrialists to compliment native whites for their good humor and willingness to work. Even today, those trapped in mundane occupations pursue them cheerfully, clerks in stores greeting female shoppers as "honey," attendants at service stations and checkers in supermarkets bidding customers to "hurry back" with genuine pleasantry.

To a considerable degree white Alabamians have disciplined their violence into more acceptable channels than lynching and murder. The truculent spirit of the Scotch-Irish is far from quenched but finds release now in an obsession with football, in cheering their heroes of the big new auto racetrack near Talladega or the wrestling rings of Birmingham as well as through age-old outlets like hunting or wagering on a surreptitious cockfight. Younger people have accommodated themselves with considerable ease to the racial revolution wrought during the 1950s and 1960s. Many older whites, without forgiving the federal government for its role, have accepted the new ways with a tolerance which even they find astounding. They work alongside blacks and share the same rest rooms, bus seats, and housing projects in apparent harmony, even violating an old taboo by sitting down to lunch at the same cafeteria table with black co-workers. Given further insight into their history, whites may come to understand that their economic and political leaders often cried "nigger" in the past to divert them onto snipe hunts and away from costly desires like higher wages, unionization, more social services, and better education for their children.

Toward this latter goal, Alabama is still engaged in a desperate race to catch up with richer states. This is a state where pioneer white children learned as best they could amid the noisy cacophony of "blab" schools, where antebellum black children learned not at all, and where the legislature, finally creating a public school system in 1854, set up a budget of $1.33 per year for each student. Victimized by the stingy attitude of Bourbon leaders toward paying for social services, citizens of many rural communities in the late nineteenth century raised what money they could to support "subscription" schools and secured a teacher by offering to let her "board around" with nearby families. After school hours the teacher was expected to help earn her keep by pitching in with chores. Sallie West, required to deworm a tobacco patch in return for her keep, never forgot her distaste for the "big, beautiful, repulsive worms." [94] Such teachers attended school themselves for six weeks or so each year (often requiring fifteen or twenty years to earn a college degree), while their students went into the fields to chop, hoe, or pick. Even today some Alabama schools start in sultry August so that children can be released to help pick the fall crops.

Oldtimers reminisce nostalgically of one-room schoolhouses with potbellied stoves to ward off winter drafts and of recess when lunch was produced from syrup buckets, boys roughhoused at leapfrog and town ball, and girls engaged in such demure games as "pass the thimble" and "pretty bits in my cup." But the one-room schoolhouse is also a symbol of educational malnutrition, a deficiency which has had long-term effect in Alabama. There is an old folktale about a fellow who boasted after

94. Elliott, *Annals of Northwest Alabama*, 3: 112.

raising his kids: "Ain't nun of 'em gone to school but nary one starved to death." [95] Yet most farm folk desperately wanted something more for their children. A. A. Self of Hanceville remembered well his mother's habit of tearing a page out of the *Blue Back Speller* each day, tacking it on a board, and hanging it around his neck until he had mastered all the words.

Even though Alabama has no heritage of public education comparable to that of New England, the Middle West, or California, some first-class minds have emerged from plain Alabama origins. In the legal field the most notable example in this century was Supreme Court Justice Hugo Black, whose father was a furnishing merchant in Ashland. Fifth District Federal Judge Frank M. Johnson, Jr., came from a long line of Republicans and Unionists in northwest Alabama and, like Black, has stuck to his concepts of justice despite furious onslaughts of wrath from his own kind. Howell Heflin, a progressive-minded nephew of "Cotton Tom," did much to reform Alabama's antiquated legal machinery in his tenure as chief justice of the Alabama Supreme Court. Out of these same ranks have come governors attuned to the moods of plain folk, James E. Folsom and George and Lurleen Wallace, and United States Senator John Sparkman, who entered the Senate as a New Dealer and whose long tenure in the upper chamber enabled him to occupy the imposing chair of the Senate Committee on Foreign Relations.

Intellectualism is still the exception rather than the rule in Alabama even though its citizens have a vast respect for the college degree as the surest ticket to upward mobility. During the administrations of George and Lurleen Wallace this enthusiasm was rewarded by an ever-growing educational appropriation, a profusion of junior colleges and trade schools, and a rush on the part of the onetime teachers' colleges to proclaim themselves universities. Educational excellence is still a distant grail but most Alabamians are pleased if not amazed at how far they have come in pursuit of it.

Typical Alabamians of the 1970s, like Hezekiah Massey in

---

95. Dodd, *Winston County*, p. 31.

the mid-1800s, are little inclined to venture far from home. Although many have been forced to leave the state for military service or to seek higher wages, few expatriates ever truly regard Michigan or California as home. Those who have remained in Alabama feel sustained by a continuing strong tie to their church, by the presence of a large contingent of relatives (the nuclear family being more typical among newcomers from other regions than among native Alabamians), by a sense of deep roots and an attachment to place, and by the comfortable assurance that they are surrounded by others who share their predominant values.

From Frederick Olmsted to Clarence Cason, sensitive observers have taken note of a further characteristic which tends to set the average white Alabamian somewhat apart from the feverish American mainstream. In his travels through northern Alabama, Olmsted came upon a simple coal digger who assured him "if you want to fare well in this country, stop to poor folks' housen; they try to enjoy what they've got while they kin." [96] Eighty years later Clarence Cason commented that his fellow Alabamians, despite their proclivity for work, were always tempted to truancy. He observed that they were less obsessed than eastern folk with the urge to improve their earthly station and therefore they had attained, without conscious effort, a serenity for which all people strive. "They can endure peace," Cason concluded.

Descendants of Ma and Pa, tolerably well-fixed now compared to the past but clinging stubbornly to many of the old ways, are still (as W. J. Cash described typical white southerners forty years ago) a curious admixture of eternally warring elements, the last American Puritans and at the same time hedonists, ever tempted to sneak away for a spell of fishing or a taste of some forbidden fruit.

96. Olmsted, *Journey in the Back Country*, p. 211.

2

Seen through a Glass, Darkly: The Tribulations of Blacks

For now we see through a glass, darkly, but then face to face.

—1 Corinthians 13:12

*O*THER migrants who had no choice as to their destination and no dreams of landowning also streamed into Alabama in the great migration which followed the War of 1812. The same British traveller who had observed the rush of farm folk toward this promised land also noted slaves being shepherded by their owners along the rough trail to Montgomery. In one day alone he saw almost a thousand male slaves "trudging on foot and worn down with fatigue," and wagons filled with females and young slaves "slowly dragging on and frequently breaking down." [1] Early one morning he came upon a professional slave trader preparing his coffle to travel, women and children clinging to the last warmth of the fire, manacled and chained men awaiting the order to set forth on a day's march which might cover twenty-five miles.

Such coffles made their appearances at the large slave marts

1. Posey, *Alabama in the 1830s*, p. 30.

in Huntsville, Montgomery, and Selma or in the squares of little Black Belt towns like Livingston and Eutaw. Mobile, the destination of many human cargoes shipped down the Mississippi or along the eastern seaboard and Gulf of Mexico, was the busiest slave market in the state. This wholesale transplanting of blacks from older states (plus an unknown number smuggled from Africa) ushered in the era of widespread plantation slavery in Alabama.

Slavery has recently come under fresh scrutiny by historians inspired by the civil rights movement of the 1960s to re-examine the roots of American racism. Younger scholars, challenging older interpretations, stirred an academic hornets' nest. On occasion professors fell to name-calling, tossing scholarly barbs like "southern apologist" and "neo-abolitionist" at one another.

Time on the Cross, a reinterpretation based upon statistics, and *Roll, Jordan, Roll,* drawn from personal accounts by slaves, their owners, and their contemporaries, attracted the widest attention. Robert W. Fogel and Stanley L. Engerman, authors of *Time on the Cross,* were booed, picketed, and vilified for claiming that the material lot of slaves compared favorably with that of free industrial workers and that the extent of slave breeding, sexual exploitation, and family separation had been exaggerated. Eugene Genovese, a self-styled Marxist, continued to pursue his class interpretation of the antebellum South and his views of paternalistic slavery. "[Genovese's] *Roll, Jordan, Roll* defies labelling," a fellow historian observed wryly, "and is calculated to drive a true Marxist out of his mind." [2]

John W. Blassingame, a black historian, also advanced startling new theories, arguing that the slave community regarded house servants as "Aunt Jemimas" and "Uncle Toms" rather than as black aristocrats, preferred conjurers to preachers, and mistrusted rather than envied the "yellow folks," many of

2. See Robert William Fogel and Stanley L. Engerman, *Time on the Cross: The Economics of American Negro Slavery* (Boston-Toronto: Little Brown and Company, 1974); Eugene D. Genovese, *Roll, Jordan, Roll: The World the Slaves Made* (New York: Random House, 1974). The comment on Genovese's work was made by Prof. Kenneth M. Stampp at a symposium on slavery in Oxford, Miss., in October 1975.

whom, he said, hated their white fathers. William Scarborough, a white historian, rose to the defense of Old Master, depicting him as a devout gentleman who sought to enforce strict discipline by means short of cruelty and evinced sincere, not merely economic, concern for the well-being of "my people." [3] Kenneth Stampp, surveying the lively disagreement among his colleagues, observed that never had so many historians concerned themselves over slavery and never had they been so far from consensus. Stampp was quick to add however that constant revision was the most enduring trait of his profession and controversy its lifeblood.

Yet in Alabama, where intellectual exchange is not common sport, black and white alike have had little exposure to recent scholarship about the subject which haunts their history most persistently. The only study of Alabama slavery was published in 1950. Its author, a white Alabamian, was a trained scholar but occasionally he exhibited a white southerner's viewpoint, as exemplified in this excerpt: "In some ways, the Negro had the best of it [slavery]. His master furnished all the necessities of life and shouldered all the worries." [4] The white author of another state history, published in 1934 but still a standard source, summed up his findings thus: "The masses of slaves seemed contented and carefree and were sentimentally attached to their masters and the plantation." [5] In one Alabama history textbook used throughout the state for years, high school students were informed that slavery was "the earliest form of social security." [6]

No black historian of the stature of John Hope Franklin or John Blassingame has yet emerged from Alabama origins. But a

3. See John W. Blassingame, *The Slave Community: Plantation Life in the Antebellum South* (New Jersey: Oxford University Press, 1972); William K. Scarborough, *The Overseer: Plantation Management in the Old South* (Baton Rouge: Louisiana State University Press, 1966).

4. James Benson Sellers, *Slavery in Alabama* (University, Ala.: University of Alabama Press, 1950), p. 80.

5. Moore, *History of Alabama*, p. 367.

6. Charles Summersell, *Alabama History for Schools* (Birmingham: Colonial Press, 1957), p. 233.

body of evidence about Alabama slavery from the black view-point does exist. The *Slave Narratives* are recollections gathered from aged black men and women during the 1930s by inter-viewers from the Federal Writers Project of the Works Progress Administration.[7] Until recently this source was disdained or ne-glected by historians who felt that memory was bound to be dimmed by the passage of more than seventy years and that these accounts were hearsay, most of them gathered by southern whites whose approach often betrayed paternalism or racism. Efforts by interviewers to reproduce black dialect offended and confused many readers.

Scholars were also wary because this project took place in the midst of the Great Depression when blacks might be more likely to appreciate the fact that some type of food, shelter, and medi-cine had been provided under slavery. A few ex-slaves in Ala-bama betrayed this unconscious influence. Of basic needs, one said: "Now us has to scuffle and git dem de bes' way we can." Another found the 1930s to be harder times than slavery when at least he had something to eat and worried only about being whipped. "Dey beats folks now," he reasoned, "so what's de difference?" But even though the hardships of the depression may have tempered their recollection of bondage, most narrators painted a dark picture of slavery.

Interviewers questioned former slaves about housing, food, work, and religion; their feelings toward master, mistress, and overseer, and their memories of songs, ghost stories, supersti-tions, slave patrols, Yankees, and the Klan. Opinion may have depended upon whether an ex-slave had been house servant or field hand or how free the narrator felt to give a forthright an-swer to a white interviewer. Such a response as "we-alls had a good time an' us was happy an' secure" may have been calcu-lated to please the white folk but even in the timid racial climate of the 1930s other Alabama blacks made bold to say: "I hope

7. Unless otherwise noted, all direct quotations on the topic of slavery in this chapter are drawn from the Alabama interviews in a microfilmed copy of Federal Writers Proj-ect, *Slave Narratives: A Folk History of Slavery in the United States From Interviews with Former Slaves* (Washington: Library of Congress, 1941). The original interviews are in the Alabama Department of Archives and History, Montgomery.

dey don't have no more such [slavery] 'cause hit was terrible,''
or ''it's bad to belong to folks dat own you soul and body. . . .
dem days was hell.''

Although the *Narratives* present many problems for interpret-
ers, they have finally been rescued from dusty oblivion in the
Library of Congress and scrutinized for evidence of the lives
and spirit of American slaves. Such a notable scholar as
C. Vann Woodward has conceded that the *Narratives* are no
more flawed than sources which historians traditionally consult
such as the newspapers, diaries, letters, speeches, and documents of whites. Woodward has urged historians to bring their
buckets to this well. Many other scholars have demonstrated
that the *Narratives,* if used with caution and checked against additional sources, can produce intimate and moving insights into
a shadowy world.

The *Narratives,* a source almost totally ignored by the writers
and teachers of Alabama history, afford glimpses of the "peculiar institution" as seen from the quarters instead of the Big
House. On many points, the accounts of slaves and masters concur. But ex-slaves offer other testimony which challenges many
of the comfortable concepts held by white Alabamians.

How was it to be a slave? Historians concede that there will
never be a "definitive" answer to this question; even the *Narratives* contain conflicting accounts. But Alabama's general impression of slavery has been shaped almost entirely by whites,
drawing primarily upon sources compiled by members of their
race. It would seem imperative that future students also weigh
the testimony of some of those who were slaves themselves. In
a chapter devoted to the black experience, it would seem fitting
to hear the voices of black Alabamians.

Being only a sampling, the *Narratives* provide no reliable statistics as to what proportion of slaves came with owners, what
percentage with speculators, and what number of slave families
became separated by auctions, but they do contain poignant
memories of the internal slave trade. A number of Alabama narrators recalled having been brought in droves from the Carolinas
or Virginia by speculators who chained likely runaways to trees

or wagon wheels at night. Reuben Fitzpatrick of Bullock County remembered that a speculator instructed him to appear "spry and fidgety" on the block and that when the auctioneer cried "Who'll bid? Who'll bid?" prospective purchasers peered into his mouth as if he were a horse. Siney Bonner, reared at Pickensville, recounted the anecdote that his father had been named "Green" Bonner because a new owner had paid $1,000 for him in Mobile. Another remembered the rueful words of this slave ditty:

> Up and down de Mobile Ribber
> Two speckerlaters for one po' lil nigger.

Laura Clark said that she was parted at the age of six from her mother in North Carolina to be sold anew in Alabama. She quoted her mother's plea to the trader: "Take keer my baby chile (dat was me) and iffen I never sees her no mo', raise her for God." Then her mother fell from the wagon in which children were being carted away and "rolled on de' groun' jes' a cryin'." But Laura and her fellow passengers had been given a rare treat of candy and could not comprehend why their relatives should weep.

Angie Garrett remembered a free black who incurred such heavy debt that he was forced to sell his five sons for cash in front of the Livingston post office. Although most historians believe that plantations devoted to slave breeding were rare, Mandy McCullough Cosby said that she had been reared in Chambers County by a master who bred slaves for the market. She recalled that her mistress cried when children were sold but that her master just laughed and went about his business. He treated his property so well that neighbors joked about "Mc-Cullough's free niggers" but Mandy Cosby, reflecting on her childhood, reasoned: "Dey gits good care for de marster expects dey will bring good money."

Descriptions of slave cabins generally concur with the accepted version of a one-room log or plank structure (16 feet by 18 feet being a common size) in which a family of five or six slept, sometimes cooked, sought shelter from inclement weather, and found a modicum of privacy. In size, furnishing, and design, these slave cabins seem strikingly similar to the first crude homes of white pioneers. Many contained "Alabama bedsteads," one end embedded in the clay of the wall, the frames corded with rope and covered with corn shucks, pine straw, moss, or cotton bolls. (Nonetheless a former slave remembered that such beds felt "lak tables.") Masters occasionally ordered slaves to scrub and whitewash their cabins for the sake of appearance, health, and sanitation. Even so one former inhabitant told her interviewer bluntly: "Dey wasn't fitten for nobody to live in. We jes' had to put up wid 'em."

Confirming the accounts left by their masters, ex-slaves described their clothing as having been made from osnaburg, a cheap form of woven cotton which could be dyed with copperas or tobacco and peach leaves. Women who worked in the fields recalled the pantalettes which they wore to keep early morning dew off their legs. Children frequently ran naked or were clothed until puberty in a one-piece garment which inspired the expression "shirttail niggers." Blacks had other vivid memories which appear in no plantation record book. The rough brogans which they called "Jackson ties," "red russets," or "nigger shoes" rubbed blisters and seldom became softened until worn out; even then such shoes could hardly be bent by the human hand. One woman split her shoes up the side so that she could move in a hurry. To improve the appearance of their shoes for Sunday wear, some slaves polished these "Jackson ties" with hog gristle or hung them over the cabin chimney until they were blackened by soot.

The *Narratives* also verify the general conclusion that slaves, being valuable, received prompt although primitive medical attention. Some remembered that medicine had been forced down their throats when a master thought it necessary. Like white pioneers they concocted their own remedies: Jerusalem weed made into candy or tea to cure worms; horehound and mullen tea for colds; foul-smelling bags of asafetida hung around their necks in hope of warding off measles, smallpox, and other mysterious ailments. Several described a procedure called "cupping" in which the doctor opened the nape of the neck with a knife and withdrew almost a quart of blood. Such bleeding was believed to rid the body of poisons which might cause dysentery, cholera, or pleurisy. Adeline Hodges of Mobile remembered that cupping and bleeding were usually followed by a dose of calomel and, next morning, a bowl of gruel. "Den us'd be all right," she said. But Adeline Hodges was evidently made of sterner stuff than others who were hastened to the grave by this drastic treatment.

Perhaps in contrast to the lean pickings of the Great Depression, ex-slaves seemed to remember their food with genuine nostalgia. The usual ration, distributed to each slave once a week, was accurately recalled as three pounds of hog meat and a peck of cornmeal. Sweet potatoes, sorghum, and buttermilk were sometimes added. Sunday might bring a special treat of sugar, coffee, and enough flour and lard to make a batch of biscuits. Many confirmed that their owners permitted them to raise greens, onions, corn, and other vegetables in small gardens near their cabins and that they further varied their basic diet by hunting opossum, rabbit, coon, or wild game at night and by fishing for trout, jack, gar, and carp. At the annual festival of hog killing they welcomed such leavings as heads, jowls, chitlings, feet, livers, and "lights."

Midday meals were usually cooked in a central kitchen and taken to the fields by a "trash gang" of children too young to work. "Mules be eatin' and niggers be eatin' " as Angie Garrett described it. In the plantation nursery younger children, using wooden spoons, fed themselves corn bread and buttermilk from open troughs on the ground. At the summons "Chillun, chillun, bread!" one remembered, "we jest burnt de wind gettin' dere." Supper, a less important meal, was cooked in the cabin fireplace or during the heat of summer on iron pots hung by sticks over a common fire in the yard. Many ex-slaves described with gusto the flavor of ash cakes or hard cornpone, wrapped in shucks or hickory leaves and cooked in the ashes, and of turnip greens and "poke sallet" boiled in an iron pot with a slab of "fat back" pork.

To this point the slave account varies only slightly from that told by their owners save for an occasional mutter that cabins "wasn't fitten for nobody to live in," that "nigger shoes" tor-

tured the feet, and that "dem days was hell." The subject of
work, however, evoked eloquent memories and betrayed a hidden strain of protest. The long work week, sunup to sundown
for six days unless a lenient master called a halt at 4:00 P.M. on
Saturdays, began before dawn with a rap on the door or the
sound of a horn, trumpet, or piece of sheet iron beaten with a
stick. During the surcease of laying-by time, field hands might
be allowed to "jubilate." In winter there were lighter tasks such
as repairing fences, weaving cloth, and tending livestock. During the hottest months, many owners decreed a midday rest
period of two hours or more. But when cotton was ready for
picking in the fall, field hands sometimes worked by candlelight,
jacklight, or moonlight. "Dere warn't so much foolishness at
cotton pickin' time," one remembered.

Even the statistical historians who offer a less stringent view
of slavery estimate that 80 per cent of women were field hands.
Mary Ella Granberry, raised on a plantation near Sheffield,
could not 'recall when she was too young to work: "Eber since I
kin 'member, I had a water bucket on my arm totin' water to de
hands. Iffen I wasn't doin' dat, I was choppin' cotton." Martha
Bradley had reached the age of 100 despite the fact that as a
young woman she had hauled logs out of the fields by straps attached to her arms. Mothers were usually summoned from the
field several times a day to suckle their fretful babies. But Sara
Colquitt recalled that she had taken her baby to the fields and
tied him to a tree limb, out of reach of ants and bugs, while she
worked the furrows. Oliver Bell of Livingston remembered that
his mother, a plowhand, left him in the shade of a post oak:
"Dere I sat all day an' dat tree was my nurse." The leisure of
childhood ended at nine or ten when young blacks joined their
elders in the fields. Walter Calloway, reared near Snowdoun,
was a regular plowhand by the age of ten.

Historians agree that whipping was a common form of punishment and work incentive in the eighteenth and early nineteenth centuries, not only on southern plantations but in other
parts of the United States, the British navy, and the coal mines
of Germany. But they debate hotly as to what degree of sadism
was intermingled with disciplinary measures on the plantation.

Many narrators who were field hands in Alabama testify that the lash was used to step up work as well as to punish the disobedient. Strong workers set the pace of hoeing and picking. "De bigges' thang dat us was punish for," recalled Mary Ella Granberry, "was not keepin' up." But Jake Green of Livingston described four hoe hands on his master's plantation who were never whipped because they could chop as fast as a mule could plow: "Whenever dey's stop at twelve o'clock, dem niggers was right dere to lay de hoe handle on de plow, an' dat's choppin'!"

According to the Alabama *Narratives* the whip was usually wielded by an overseer although some former slaves recalled harsh black "drivers" and stern masters. Several remembered overseers who dictated that salt and pepper be rubbed into their raw wounds. "An' they'd as well get on to work quick," one narrator said, "cause they can't be still nohow." One said that slaves on his plantation secretly referred to the overseer by his first name because they "hated to 'mister' that man."

Carrie Davis of Smith's Station told her interviewer that slaves on a neighboring plantation were whipped with a strap which had holes in it, raising blisters which were then cut open with a handsaw and washed in saltwater. When victims of these whippings came to plead for water, her sympathetic mistress also gave them salve. Mingo White of Franklin County ventured the opinion: "Dey don't 'low a man to whup a horse lack dey whupped us in dem days."

"Breeder women," who delivered a child every twelve months "like a cow bringin' in a calf," were usually spared the whip. But the *Narratives* contain one searing account of a black driver who placed a pregnant woman, stomach down, in a hole and whipped her until her baby dropped onto the ground. Amy Chapman, a slave on one of the absentee plantations owned by Reuben Chapman, governor of Alabama from 1847 to 1849, said that she had been stripped naked and whipped by a cat-o'-nine-tails wielded by an overseer. As a boy, Oliver Bell watched as an overseer ordered his mother stripped to the waist and beaten with a leather strap. When he wept, "Mistis Beckie said, 'Go git dat boy a biskit.' "

Some slaves sought revenge on hated overseers or attempted to escape. When an overseer whipped Martha Bradley, she bit and kicked him until he released her. "I didn't know no better then," she recollected. After the overseer of another plantation fell ill, slaves believed that they had "hoodooed" him. But he recovered and returned to the fields, shouting: "You thought you had ole Buck but by God he rose again!" This narrator remembered that "niggers were so skeered that they squatted in the fields like partridges." One former slave recounted the story of a black man who was burned alive after he killed his overseer. But another told of the dramatic retribution exacted by a runaway slave named Jake. Tracked down and treed by "nigger dogs," Jake recognized his pet redbone Belle among the barking pack. When the overseer climbed the tree to fetch his quarry, Jake kicked him to the ground, yelling "Hol'im, Belle!" Following Belle's example, the pack chewed the overseer to death while Jake made his getaway.

Another man also named Jake had no such luck in attempting to escape. He had been the best blacksmith in his county and, like many other spirited and talented slaves, chafed under bondage. One night he stole into the forbidden confines of his mistress's bedroom and took her moneybag to buy his way north. Jake was caught and whipped so fiercely that he died three days later. Caroline Holland, who recounted this story, concluded: "Jake jus' had too big ideas fo' a nigger."

Forms of punishment more fearful than the whip were recalled by other Alabama ex-slaves. If charged with serious infractions, they were confined in the "calaboose," "sweat box," or "nigger box." One described the "nigger box" as barely large enough for a prisoner to stand erect and lighted only by air holes to prevent suffocation; those imprisoned were fed only water and cornbread made without salt. Another reported: "Iffen you had done a bigger' nough thang, you was kep' in the de nigger box for months at a time an' when you got out you was nothin' but skin and bones an' scurcely able to walk."

But interviewers also found evidence that some Alabama planters encouraged work by positive incentives, a system noted by Genovese and the statistical historians. A woman in Fairhope recalled that she was once given 100 pounds of cotton as reward for picking 480 pounds in one day, a feat by which she outperformed a male rival. Four hoe hands who could pick a bale a day were once rewarded with 500 pounds of cotton apiece.

Most of those who served in the Big House appear to have been spared the whip. In their interviews they evince a devotion to their white families which, Blassingame contends, caused less privileged slaves to regard them with suspicion. An old black man who spoke wistfully of the days when he drove his master's rig "amongst de Eufaula high steppers" may well have been considered an "Uncle Tom" by fellow slaves. Genovese credits house servants with a strong sense of racial identification but he too found that they sometimes displayed caste feelings. Matilda Pugh Daniel appears to have scorned some of her own race. She enjoyed her status as house servant to the family of James L. Pugh of Eufaula, who became a United States senator after the Civil War, and proudly described how she had washed the julep glasses, polished the silver, and worn "Miss Sara's" white tarleton dress with a pink bow in front when she got married. "I ain't neber 'sociated with no trashy niggers," Matilda Daniel said, "an' I ain't neber inten' to."

Emma Thomas was trained in fine sewing, setting the table, and serving guests at dinner parties so deftly that they were scarcely aware of her presence. To master the latter art she practiced blindfolded. On occasion her owner, Judge F. G. Kimball of Mobile, asked her to blindfold herself and demonstrate her skill to amuse his guests. Judge Kimball also insisted that his house servants speak correct English. If Emma replied, "I ain't comin'," she said that her owner chastised her until she rephrased an answer such as "I shan't do it."

Some former house servants described duties no more onerous than sleeping on a pallet or trundle bed in case the white children needed anything at night or keeping flies off the mistress with a turkey feather fan. But others told of harsh experiences as house servants. Delia Garlic said that a former mistress seared her arm with a hot iron because she had allowed a white baby to incur a slight hurt. One of Delia's later mis-

tresses, discovering that her slave had put "smut" on her eye-
brows as white women sometimes did, hit her with a piece of
stovewood and yelled: "You black devil, I'll show you to mock
your betters." Mingo White reported that his mother's tasks
were to cook for all the field hands, serve as maid to the master's daughter, spin and card four "cuts" of thread a day (143
threads to a cut), and wash and iron all clothes on Wednesdays.
If she failed to perform any one of these tasks she was given
fifty lashes. Her son recalled that his mother dared to threaten
the master during one whipping: "Lay it on, Marsa White,
'caze I'm goin' to tell de Yankees when dey come."

The brighter moments of slavery, as pictured in the Alabama
Narratives, were Christmas, corn shuckings, hog killing time,
Saturday nights, and slave weddings. Masters of some plantations condoned Saturday night dancing and even came to watch.
Many arranged occasional corn shucking contests at which
slaves were encouraged to choose "generals" and given a jug
of liquor to spur their competition: "Den dey shore would work
and dat pile'd jus' vanish." Marriage was frequently described
as jumping over a broom, a ceremony of unknown origin. But
several narrators recalled fancy weddings in the Big House with
the master or a minister performing the ceremonies. One remarked that her master was careful about those whom his slaves
married, fearing that "light niggers" would not produce as
strong a stock as full-blooded blacks. Another said: "If marster
wanted to mix his stock of slaves wid a strong stock on another
plantation, dey would do dem mens and womens jes lak
horses."

Ex-slaves overwhelmingly agreed that education was forbidden by owners who feared that those who could read and write
would get ideas of freedom. "Iffen we was caught lookin' in a
book," said William Henry Townes of Tuscumbia, "we was
treated same as iffen we had killed somebody." Some told of
owners who whacked off a forefinger or hand of a transgressor
of this rigid rule in order to impress upon other slaves the terrible price of seeking to educate themselves. When an interviewer
asked Charlie Aaron if he had been taught to read, he replied:
"No, Madame, only to work." Younger slaves sometimes

picked up a little knowledge from an indulgent mistress or from white children who showed them pictures in their schoolbooks. One ex-slave recalled that as he carried books to school for his young master, "I would look in de book and git a little learnin'."

For fear that religious zeal might cloak plots of insurrection and escape, owners also discouraged or carefully monitored prayer meetings in the quarters. Many Alabama ex-slaves spoke of the common custom of turning a large iron washpot bottom-side upward "so sound our voices go under de pot." The sociologist George Rawick has speculated that this use of the washpot had links with the ceremonial pots of Africa or to the hollow and resonant drum forbidden in the South. Many black Alabamians remembered using the washpot to deaden noise because, as Oliver Bell put it, "dey didn't like for us to sing and pray loud in de quarters." Ned White, caught praying for freedom, was stretched between four pegs on the ground and whipped until blood ran from him "like a hog." Fellow slaves, brought to watch, were warned that this would be the fate of any caught in such a mutinous act.

White owners preferred to see their slaves neatly and safely ensconced in the balconies or back pews of their own churches. Remembering those days, Tildy Collins recalled that her hair was wrapped with thread on Sundays and twisted so tightly that she could barely shut her eyes. Mary Ella Granberry told her interviewer candidly: "Us didn't git no pleasure outten goin' to church caze we warn't lowed to say nothin'."

No Denmark Vesey or Nat Turner emerged to lead Alabama slaves to rebellion. But to ensure that blacks were not "rising" under cover of darkness each neighborhood had its patrol to monitor the countryside after the nightly curfew and to whip or imprison any black found at large without a written permit from the master. Some Alabama slaves remembered that their masters forbade "paterollers" to interfere with their coming and going but such trusting whites were in the minority. Antebellum newspapers in the Black Belt frequently reported rumors of insurrection, especially at Christmas season when most field hands were idle.

The Alabama *Narratives* contain many stories about Yankee soldiers whose mission was not clear to all slaves and whose coming often seemed to frighten blacks as much as whites. Some former house servants recounted proudly how they had helped the mistress hide family treasures. With evident amusement, Cheney Cross of Evergreen described how a Yankee, ripping open a feather mattress in search of silver, got a feather stuck in his windpipe and almost suffocated. Hannah Irwin, who lived in the small community of Louisville, remembered her astonishment when a Northern soldier, evidently seeing cotton for the first time, asked her "whut wuz dem white flowers in de field." Although they might have been mystified or terrified by Yankee soldiers, most slaves seemed to have had a clearer concept of Abraham Lincoln. "I never seed Mr. Lincoln," Angie Garrett said, "but when dey tole me 'bout him, I thought he was partly God."

Divided into owners and slaves but bound together by the intimacy of plantation life, blacks and whites developed many close ties. Even Genovese the Marxist has conceded that there were "deep and intimate friendships, if such a word may be applied to so unequal a relationship." [8] Recognizing the inherent contradiction between friendship and bondage, conscientious historians have phrased their conclusions about the slave-master relationship with prudence. Woodward has stated that "father figures and hate images" are part of the heritage from slavery. Fogel and Engerman have concluded that both cruelty and affection had their place on southern plantations. Genovese has described the Big House as a tangled web of fondness and hatred, interracial attachments and intolerance, extraordinary kindness and uncontrolled violence.

The Alabama *Narratives* attest to this same ambivalence. Glimpses of genuine affection are interwoven with tales of cruelty. Many recalled with gratitude a plantation mistress who nursed them when they were ill, read the Bible to them on Sundays, refused to allow black women to be whipped or to do heavy work like rolling logs, and wept when slaves were sold

8. Genovese, *Roll, Jordan, Roll*, p. 348.

or as she arranged the shrouds of their dead. Joseph Holmes of Pritchard said "Mistis was an angel." But other former slaves, recollecting mistresses who punished them when they did not spin or card enough thread at night or who forbade black children to call their parents "Mammy" and "Daddy," expressed no such warm affection.

Former slaves in Alabama, like the majority of those interviewed in other southern states, have more good than ill to say about Old Master. Esther Green, who said that she never saw an adult whipped, remembered how she and other black children had danced for the master's pleasure: "We sho' used to have a big time out on dem big white porches." Virginia Birdsong belonged to a master in Camden who disapproved of slavery but, being enmeshed in it, ordered that his slaves call him "Papa" instead of "Master." Emma Chapman was owned by a Baptist preacher in Pickens County who employed no overseer, permitted no whipping, and gave passes to his slaves to come and go so freely that other slaves regarded them as "free niggers." Emma Howard told her interviewer that vengeful neighbors poisoned her master because he "was too good to his niggers." Tildy Collins, a victim of the Great Depression, expressed the belief that "iffen Old Marster was livin' now, I'd be all right an' not hafter worry 'bout nuffin."

The contradictory evidence in the Alabama *Narratives* only serves to underscore Kenneth Stampp's observation that all sources on slavery are treacherous. Perhaps hidden feelings may be defined more accurately from indirect clues than from answers to prying questions about how ex-slaves regarded their owners. Ank Bishop, born in slavery and an old man during the Great Depression, gave a stark summation of his life's span:

> Bred an' bawn in Sumter County, wore out in Sumter County, 'specks to die in Sumter County, an' whut is I got? Ain't got nothin', ain't got nothin', ain't got nothin'.

There are similar glimpses of resignation and despair in songs remembered from slavery such as "Travel On, Travel On, Soon Be Over," "Hark from de Tomb a Doleful Sound," "Steal Away," and "Goin' Home to Live with the Lord." But one old

black Alabamian recalled a lyric which offered a glimmer of
hope:

> My lates sun is sinkin' fas'
> My race is nearly run
> My strongs' trial now is pas'
> My triumph jes' begun.

Guests at Judge Kimball's dinner table in Mobile, who
scarcely noticed Emma Thomas when she served them, suffered
a peculiar visual affliction. They could see fellow guests clearly
but, unless Judge Kimball called attention to her proficiency,
Emma Thomas was virtually invisible. Wherever the well-to-do
congregate, they often exhibit this social blindness toward those
who appear in the guise of servants, whether black, brown,
yellow, or white. But in the South where servant ranks have
traditionally been filled by blacks, countless Emma Thomases
have moved like umbral shadows in the background, perceived
by whites only when service is needed.

Thus it is not surprising that white Alabama historians of the
old school, reared on the plantation or steeped in its ways, also
evidenced a perceptual problem in regard to blacks. Describing
Reconstruction, they saw freedmen as stereotypes like
"darkies" and "big bucks," and showered them with adjec-
tives such as "jet black," "sable," "copper-colored,"
"burly," and "ignorant." Unaccustomed to the idea of black
political leaders, they overlooked these men altogether or
viewed them as in the distorted mirror of a carnival show.

John Witherspoon DuBose, a former planter, slaveowner, and
Klansman, mentioned Alabama's first black congressman, Benjamin Sterling Turner, by his slave name of "Ben Gee" and
paid him this patronizing compliment: "a remarkably efficient
and intelligent servant." [9] DuBose's view of Reconstruction,
capsuled in his title, *Alabama's Tragic Decade,* first appeared in
1912 as a newspaper serial and was reissued in 1940 as a book

---

9. John Witherspoon DuBose, *Alabama's Tragic Decade: Ten Years of Alabama,
1865–1874,* ed. James K. Greer (Birmingham: Webb Book Co., 1940), p. 311.

wherein blacks were cartooned as comic figures with vapid expressions and outsized lips.

Another early treatment of Alabama history, first published in 1934, still gets brisk usage by high school students in pursuit of term papers. Its author, A. B. Moore, evidently confusing Benjamin Turner with William V. Turner, a contemporary black teacher and state legislator from Wetumpka, dismissed the congressman with this phrase: "along with the native sons sent to make laws for the nation was one William Turner, a negro [*sic*]." Whether blacks became state legislators or members of Congress, the spectacle of former servants as lawmakers horrified one ex-Confederate quoted by Moore: "What right hath Dahomey [a state on the west coast of Africa] to give laws to Runnymede, or Bosworth Field to take a lesson from Congo-Ashan? Shall Bill Turner . . . give laws to the mighty [white] men of the South?" [10]

Walter Lynwood Fleming made a commendable effort, for a white Alabamian born during Reconstruction, to treat Civil War and Reconstruction in a scholarly manner. [11] But even the professionally trained Fleming, son of a planter, slaveowner, and Confederate soldier, was too touchy about Reconstruction to be free from animus and prejudice. Although Fleming's study was published in 1905, no scholar has since risen to the challenge of revising his comprehensive account of Alabama's Reconstruction to make newer views available in book form.

The task of studying black leaders like Turner has been left largely to graduate students in faraway universities whose doctoral dissertations are neither readily available nor especially palatable to a young Alabama black in search of a racial model. So Turner, James Thomas Rapier, and Jeremiah Haralson, the only blacks ever to represent Alabama in Congress, are still hazy figures in the history of their state. Any high school student, reading DuBose, Moore, or Fleming, may readily discover that Turner was "copper colored," Rapier a mulatto, and Haralson "jet black." But it is difficult to discern these men as

10. Moore, *History of Alabama,* pp. 485–486.
11. This reference is to Fleming, *Civil War and Reconstruction in Alabama.*

pioneers who, although having different philosophies and sometimes being rivals, attempted to lead their race through strange and parlous times.

Serving only one term each in Congress, Turner, Rapier, and Haralson wrote no legislation; indeed only the educated Rapier felt sufficiently self-assured to address the House. But Benjamin Turner, who rose out of slavery and illiteracy to become Dallas County tax collector, Selma city councilman, and United States Representative, deserves better than to be identified as "Ben Gee" or "William." Rapier left documents which reveal his story in more detail than that of his colleagues but no scholarly biography has yet appeared about this remarkable free black who organized the first black labor union in the South before turning to politics. Alabama history gives few glimpses of the proud, fiery Haralson, a onetime field hand, who, according to a Democratic newspaper of his day, rose to be "by far the most prominent Negro in the state." [12] The redemption of Alabama's black congressmen from obscurity and obloquy is long overdue. Fully a century after their service in Washington, they are at least entitled to be *visible* in state history.

Turner, in his brief congressional biography, stated that he was born a slave in North Carolina, brought to the Alabama Black Belt at five, and gained a "fair education" through "clandestine study." [13] Other sources claim that Turner learned little more than how to write his new name. DuBose described "Ben Gee" as "a sturdy, powerful man" who toted the baggage of white travellers from the Selma railroad station to the hotel of his owner, J. T. Gee, and, overhearing the talk of whites, gleaned a rudimentary knowledge of politics.

After the Confederacy's demise, Turner evidently prospered in his own business which he described as "mercantile" in his congressional sketch but which others have said was a livery stable. Like Rapier and Haralson, he is reported to have been

12. Samuel Denny Smith, *The Negro in Congress* (Chapel Hill: University of North Carolina Press, 1940), p. 83.

13. *Biographical Directory of the American Congress: 1774–1961* (Washington: U.S. Government Printing Office, 1961), p. 1835.

encouraged to enter politics by another dim figure, identified only as A. Forman, a shoemaker supposed to have been the first of his race to enter Alabama politics.[14]

Under the aegis of Radical Republicanism, Turner was elected to represent the First District of Alabama, comprising a large part of the Black Belt, in the Forty-Second Congress of 1871–1873. His moderate demeanor evidently pleased the native white leadership of Turner's district. In Washington Turner appears to have been a loyal Republican who attended House sessions faithfully and voted in favor of a loyalty oath for ex-Confederates, mixed schools, and civil rights for his race. Defeated in 1872 when another black candidate split the Radical vote, Turner yielded his seat to Frederick G. Bromberg of Mobile, a white Republican supported by many Democrats as well as by moderate Republicans.

James Thomas Rapier arrived in Congress via a strikingly different route. Both Fleming and Moore describe Rapier as a Canadian who, as Moore expressed it, "championed negro [sic] equality and regaled his sable friends and carpetbaggers with stories of his dining with English lords." [15] Actually Rapier, born in Lauderdale County in 1837, was the only native Alabamian of the three. Horace Mann Bond, a black scholar of Alabama Reconstruction, mistakenly identified Rapier as the offspring of a free black woman and a white planter.[16] In reality Rapier, although mulatto by ancestry, was the son of John Rapier, a free black emancipated in the 1820s by the Alabama legislature in response to a request by his owner, Richard Rapier, a Tennessee River barge captain.

The new freedman married a free black woman and became a prosperous barber known as "Uncle John" by his devoted white clients in Florence, who included Probate Judge S. C. Posey and Edward Asbury O'Neal, later to become governor of Ala-

14. Joseph M. Brittain, "Negro Suffrage and Politics in Alabama since 1870" (Ph.D. diss., University of Indiana, 1958), p. 33.

15. Fleming, *Civil War and Reconstruction*, pp. 521–523; Moore, *History of Alabama*, p. 487.

16. Horace Mann Bond, *Negro Education in Alabama: A Study in Cotton and Steel* (New York: Atheneum, 1939), p. 17.

bama. O'Neal, so one old story goes, once threatened a man who attempted to pick a fight with his barber: "I took off my coat and told the man 'if you have anything to settle with John, settle it with me'." [17]

John Rapier spent a large share of all he earned to send his four young sons out of Alabama where law specified a $500 fine for anyone teaching free blacks to spell, read, or write. Thus James attended school for seven years in Buxton, Canada, a refuge for fugitive slaves. He reported to his father that he had learned to read Greek and "knock [off] a Chapter in Caesar [in Latin] as slick as any of them." Another of John Rapier's sons became the first black admitted to the University of Michigan and earned an M.D. degree in 1864. The other sons studied in Buxton, Buffalo, and at Fisk University in Nashville. In tribute to his father's zeal, James Rapier wrote in 1862: "Father has done a man's part in educating his sons." [18]

After 1831 another Alabama law prohibited free blacks from entering the state under penalty of being sold into slavery. John Rapier could visit his sons but they dared not return to their birthplace. Safe within his Canadian sanctuary, James Rapier pledged: "If I live and God is willing, I will endeavor to do [my part] in solving the problems of [black poverty and illiteracy] in my native land." [19] His opportunity came after the Civil War when James Rapier returned to Alabama to become a successful planter. He first appeared in politics as a delegate from Lauderdale County to the Constitutional Convention of 1867 where some white delegates, unaccustomed to being challenged by blacks, characterized Rapier's speeches as "violent and highly inflammatory harangues." [20]

Later Rapier went to Washington to help organize a national

17. Loren Schweninger, "John H. Rapier, Sr.: A Slave and Freedman in the Ante-Bellum South" *Civil War History* 20 (March 1974): 23–34.

18. Schweninger, "John H. Rapier, Sr.," p. 28.

19. Loren Schweninger, "James Rapier and the Negro Labor Movement, 1869–1872," *Alabama Review,* 28, no. 3 (July 1975): 186.

20. Peter Kolchin, *First Freedom: The Responses of Alabama's Blacks to Emancipation and Reconstruction* (Westport, Conn.: Greenwood Press, 1972), p. 169.

black labor union and seek to persuade Congress to subdivide
public lands into homesteads for freedmen. Although he ob-
tained a sympathetic hearing from President U. S. Grant, he
eventually concluded that Washington's promises to black
southern laborers were empty ones and that freedmen themselves would have to demand their rights. Responding to Rapier's call, ninety-eight black farmers and laborers from forty-
two Alabama counties assembled in the house chamber at
Montgomery in 1871 to form the Labor Union of Alabama.
Jeremiah Haralson, then a state legislator from Dallas County,
was elected president.

One committee of the new union reported that the annual net
income of a black farmer in Alabama in 1869 had been
$387.13. After such a farmer purchased food, feed, medical
care, clothing, and paid interest on borrowed money, he had
nothing left from a year's hard work. Although some freedmen
sought a better life in Kansas, Rapier did not advocate emigra-
tion. He urged instead that the federal government build schools
and buy books so that black children might have better opportunity in their home state. The brief movement to unionize blacks
was doomed, however, by Republican indifference, opposition
from white landowners, and lack of federal support. Rapier
turned again to politics.

Elected Republican representative to Congress in 1872 from
the Second District, which included Montgomery, Rapier was
named to a delegation which represented the United States at the
Vienna Exposition of 1873. But once back in his native country, Representative Rapier was refused service by inns from
Montgomery to Washington and forced to share second-class
railroad cars with the riffraff. He complained bitterly to the
House: "Here I am the peer of the proudest but on a steamboat
or railroad car, I am not equal to the most degraded. Is this not
anomalous and ridiculous?" [21]

His humiliation lent eloquence to Rapier's plea for passage of
a civil rights act to guarantee equal rights for blacks in such

21. U.S., Congress, House, *Congressional Record,* 43rd. Cong., 1st session., 1874:
4782.

public places as inns, conveyances, and theaters. While this measure was being debated, a bill to plan a suitable commemoration of the centennial of the United States, born with the promise that "all men are created equal," was under consideration by the House. Such irony was not lost upon Rapier, who told his colleagues that he could not support the centennial bill:

How would I appear at the centennial celebration of our national freedom, with my own galling chains of slavery hanging about me? I could no more rejoice on that occasion in my present condition than the Jews could sing in their wonted style as they sat as captives beside the Babylonian streams. . . . I can no more forget my manhood than they could forget Jerusalem. . . . Either I am a man or I am not a man. If one, I am entitled to all the rights, privileges, and immunities common to any other class in the country.[22]

Like Turner, Rapier was defeated when he sought re-election. But Jeremiah Haralson, once sold on the auction block to a Selma owner, won a seat in Congress in 1874. Haralson had become a preacher after the Civil War, taught himself to read and write, and served in both houses of the Alabama legislature. The *Mobile Register,* although politically opposed to Haralson, described his political tactics with grudging admiration:

Jere, black as the ace of spades and with the brogue of the cornfield, ascended the rostrum. A burly Negro, shrewd and fully aware of the strength of his people, insolent to his opponents and always advancing his line of battle while professing to desire nothing but the rights of his race, uncompromising, irritating and bold. . . .[23]

One of Haralson's white Radical supporters had told a Republican meeting in Selma that it was appropriate for the Black Belt to be represented in Congress by a full-blooded black, "the blacker, the better." [24] But once in Congress, Haralson disappointed Radicals by advocating general amnesty and universal

---

22. U.S., Congress, House, *Congressional Record,* 43rd Cong., 1st session., 1874: 4784.
23. Smith, *The Negro in Congress,* p. 83.
24. Smith, *The Negro in Congress,* pp. 84–85.

suffrage in hope of bringing racial goodwill to Alabama. Defending this position against attacks by Rapier, Haralson addressed an open letter to his constituents:

> Is it not better for us in general, especially in the South, that there be good feeling between white and black? We must drive out these hell hounds and go in for peace between the two races in the South.[25]

By 1876 Alabama had been virtually "redeemed" from Reconstruction by the "white man's party," as Democrats had begun to call themselves. The legislature gerrymandered congressional districts so that no more than one, the newly created fourth, comprising most Black Belt counties, was in danger of going Republican. Feuding over their differences, Rapier and Haralson sought election to Congress from the Fourth District and split the black vote. Both were defeated by C. M. Shelley, of Selma, a former Confederate general.

After two unsuccessful attempts to regain a seat in Congress, Haralson moved to Colorado, where it was reported that he was killed by wild beasts. James Rapier was appointed to a federal job in Montgomery. After his death in 1883 he was buried in Calvary Cemetery, Saint Louis, Missouri. Benjamin Turner, whose moderation had found favor with his white constituents, was buried in a section of Selma's Live Oak Cemetery set aside for faithful servants.

James Rapier had lost his last political race while the Republican party was beginning to abandon freedmen to the political custody of their former masters. With the cause of civil rights hushed save for a few voices crying in the wilderness, Rapier faded to obscurity in the annals of his native state. But another black man whose approach to race relations would win him enduring and worldwide fame arrived in 1881 at a small Alabama town on the fringe of the Black Belt.

By contrast with Rapier, Booker Taliaferro Washington had been born in slavery and had been steeped at Hampton Institute

25. Smith, *The Negro in Congress*, p. 85.

in the values of manual labor, strict discipline, and industrial education. He applied this creed to the task of building a similar black normal school to be supported by an unlikely coalition of Alabama legislators and northern philanthropists.

Tuskegee Institute was conceived, not from philanthropic motives or a sense of *noblesse oblige,* but through an outright political bargain. Black voters of Macon County had agreed to depart from Republicanism and support an ex-Confederate Democratic candidate for the state senate in return for the candidate's promise to propose a tax-supported normal school in the county for blacks. By trading political independence for educational and economic gain, these black voters set an example of pragmatic compromise which Booker T. Washington was quick to emulate.

To become acquainted with his adopted state the young principal travelled for a month through rural Alabama, slept in one-room cabins which sheltered entire families, and shared their fat pork, corn bread, and black-eyed peas. He observed with dismay that their cotton was mortgaged, their children often dirty or naked, and their prospect of escape from the mire of poverty virtually nonexistent. Washington also visited remote schools held in churches or log cabins, equipped only with crude blackboards, and presided over by ill-prepared black teachers whose pay was less than one dollar a day. In one such school he found five students studying from a single textbook.

His tour reinforced Washington's determination to model Tuskegee, not upon the Latin schools of New England, but upon Hampton: "To take the children of such people . . . and give them a few hours of book learning would be almost a waste of time." [26] Writing his autobiography years later, Washington recalled that one of the most hopeless sights he had seen during his first tour of Alabama was a bedraggled black youth studying French grammar in a one-room cabin. W. E. B. DuBois, the black intellectual who was to become Washington's severest critic, was horror-struck by this limited vision of educational

---

26. Booker T. Washington, *Up from Slavery: An Autobiography* (Garden City, N.Y.: Doubleday and Company, 1963), p. 85.

opportunity. "One wonders," DuBois wrote, "what Socrates and St. Francis of Assisi would say to this." [27]

Washington's concept of education appealed however to both northern and southern whites. His diligent quest of financial support eventually attracted more philanthropists to Tuskegee Institute than to Hampton. Although sons and daughters of black tenants and sharecroppers occasionally rebelled at chores like brickmaking or erecting buildings, and some of his faculty chafed at Washington's preference for industrial training over liberal arts, Tuskegee was not to alter its emphasis until long after the death of its founder.

As absolutely as Old Master had ruled his plantation, Washington dominated his campus, reprimanding students for every missing button or torn sleeve, enforcing toothbrushing and the daily bath, and tolerating little or no dissent by his academic colleagues. His most famous faculty member, the black agricultural chemist George Washington Carver, shared his leader's approach to racial matters, proving so deferential to whites that, as one historian put it, he "out-Bookered" Booker Washington.[28]

In Alabama, Washington allied himself with paternalistic planters and businessmen rather than with poorer whites or more restive blacks. By stressing industrial education he won the support of powerful men who otherwise might have opposed higher education for blacks. To maintain Tuskegee's favored position with the Alabama legislature he courted such conservative leaders as Publisher W. W. Screws of the *Montgomery Advertiser* and Governors Edward A. O'Neal (1882–1886) and Thomas G. Jones (1890–1894). It was Washington who persuaded President Theodore Roosevelt to nominate Jones, a corporation attorney twice elected governor despite the Populist challenge of Reuben F. Kolb, to become federal district judge for northern Alabama.

Washington's influence extended far beyond the borders of

27. W.E.B. DuBois, *The Souls of Black Folk* (New York: New American Library, Signet Classic, 1969), p. 81.

28. Louis R. Harlan, *Booker T. Washington: The Making of a Black Leader, 1856*–1901 (New York: Oxford University Press, 1972), pp. 276–277.

ALABAMA

A photographer's essay by Bruce Roberts

REVIVAL
NOW IN PROGRESS
NITELY·7:15

Photographs in sequence

Guntersville Lake, near state park, Huntsville.
State Capitol, Montgomery.
High-rise building, downtown Birmingham.
Battleship *Alabama*, now a war memorial, Mobile.
Fishing boats at Dauphin Island.
Moon-buggy and rockets at Marshall Space Center, Huntsville.
Church, downtown Birmingham.
Tent revival near Birmingham.
Crop duster in cockpit, central Alabama.
Lunchroom at Hazel Green, north of Huntsville.
Steelworker, Birmingham.
Inside State Capitol, Montgomery.
Crossroads store, south Alabama.
Auto mall, downtown Birmingham.
Cattle grazing in pecan orchard, central Alabama.

Alabama and the realm of education. A tireless and highly successful fund-seeker, he was favorably received by such moguls as Andrew Carnegie, Collis P. Huntingdon, H. H. Rogers, and Julius Rosenwald. He bossed the so-called Tuskegee Machine which comprised a large segment of the "talented tenth" of northern black professional elite. With such a following of influential whites and blacks, Washington inevitably attracted the attention of presidents. Both William McKinley and Theodore Roosevelt made pilgrimages to Tuskegee. Roosevelt even invited Washington to share the White House dinner table with Mrs. Roosevelt, Alice, and the three Roosevelt sons, an unprecedented gesture in 1901 which aroused a brief furor.

Booker T. Washington had vaulted to national leadership by his famous advice, delivered at the Atlanta Exposition of 1895, that southerners of both races should "cast down your buckets where you are." He assured whites that they would find their former slaves patient and unresentful and promised blacks that they would be rewarded by jobs and economic opportunity. Seeking to put the old specter of social equality to rest, Washington held his hand high above his head, stretched the fingers apart to illustrate social separation, then clenched his fist to demonstrate interracial unity in the search for material progress. But implicit in the Atlanta Compromise was an understanding that blacks, if fairly treated in other areas, would not press for social, political, nor legal rights. Such privileges, Washington said, "will come to us as the result of severe and constant struggle rather than artificial forcing." [29]

These vital concessions did not pass unchallenged. John Hope, president of Atlanta University, replied, "we demand social equality," and, as if echoing James Rapier, "we shall be men." [30] DuBois, like Rapier born free and educated in the classical tradition, wrote in rebuttal:

. . . the way for a people to gain their reasonable rights is not by voluntarily throwing them away and insisting that they do not want them. . . . On the contrary, Negroes must insist continually, in

29. Harlan, *Booker T. Washington*, pp. 217–219.

30. Daniel Walden, "The Contemporary Opposition to the Political and Educational Ideas of Booker T. Washington," *Journal of Negro History* 45: (April 1960): 108–109.

season and out of season, that voting is necessary to modern manhood, that color discrimination is barbarism, and that black boys need education as well as white boys.[31]

In the 1930s the black educator Horace Mann Bond, after a careful study of black schooling in Alabama, concluded that Washington had made little progress toward transforming rural schools or creating a settled class of landowning black farmers. But Bond did credit Washington with immeasurable achievement in encouraging private philanthropy and conceded the intangible influence of his "vivid, towering personality" upon "the slow and sub-surface movements of human events." "And who," Bond asked, "shall deny the importance of legends as social forces in affecting the course of human history?" [32]

Ironically Tuskegee, which won world renown because it offered vocational opportunity to children of the poor, became a status symbol to ambitious blacks who had little or no interest in vocational education. Middle-class Alabama blacks, who struggled to afford a Tuskegee education for their sons and daughters, wanted them trained, not in brickmaking, but in the liberal arts or for professions such as nursing, veterinary medicine, and social work.

In the 1950s Tuskegee's emphasis began to shift even more definitely toward the liberal arts. Although it continued to attract many poor blacks, the majority of its students came from middle-class backgrounds. Trades like tailoring and dressmaking were dropped from the curriculum. It was left to smaller schools like Snow Hill Institute in Wilcox County and Street Manual Training School at Richmond, Alabama, to carry on Washington's tradition.

Ironically too, the civil rights victories of the mid-twentieth century hurt rather than helped Tuskegee by opening the doors of formerly all-white universities to black students and placing a premium upon qualified black academicians. Proud Tuskegee was forced to compete both to attract students and to retain the cream of its faculty. Although it still received a measure of sup-

---

31. DuBois, *Souls of Black Folk,* p. 91.
32. Bond, *Negro Education in Alabama,* pp. 222–225.

port from the Alabama legislature, Tuskegee by 1976 was experiencing the same financial deprivation as many other universities dependent largely on private funds.

Washington's stature, too, diminished in contrast with that of civil rights activists whose determined tactics won major breakthroughs in the 1950s and 1960s. But many older blacks in his adopted state still revere their early leader. A. G. Gaston was an impressionable youth of eighteen when he read *Up from Slavery* and heard the legendary Washington speak at a black church in Birmingham. "He . . . held me transfixed," Dr. Gaston wrote fifty years later when he enjoyed the status of being Alabama's most successful black businessman and had christened some of his major enterprises after Booker T. Washington.[33] As the seal of their approbation, white Alabamians enshrined Washington as the only black face in their state's hall of fame.

After studying Washington's complex personality for years, his biographer Louis R. Harlan concluded that this was no philosopher but a man of action, willing to don any mask to achieve immediate goals. Although appearing humble and deferential as a fund-raiser in both the North and South, the principal of Tuskegee ruled as a benevolent despot on the grounds of his school. While serving as machine boss over northern black intelligentsia and business leaders, he presented himself to southern blacks as a kindly father who exhorted them to seek no more than industrial skills and a peasant economy. Behind the guise of a black leader who accepted segregation and abjured militancy, Washington covertly supplied money to finance legal challenges to Jim Crow transportation, peonage, and the denial of jury service and voting rights to his race. Confounded by such a "behavioral riddle," Harlan compared Washington to "a minotaur, a lion, a fox, or Brer Rabbit . . . . a personality that had vanished into the roles it played." [34] In any guise he assumed, Booker T. Washington single-mindedly pursued the

---

33. A.G. Gaston, *Green Power* (Birmingham: Southern University Press, 1968), p. 26.

34. Harlan, *Booker T. Washington,* p. ix.

power to lead his race—but at a cautious pace and along whatever narrow path he deemed best.

Violence, the hasty recourse for settling scores between white men in frontier Alabama, was focused upon blacks after emancipation and war had proclaimed them to be people instead of property. The old midnight fear that slaves were "rising" gave way to apprehension that armed freedmen would ravish the countryside. In response, the Klan terrorized and flogged untold numbers of ex-slaves. Other self-anointed regulators, posing as Men of Justice, Order of Peace, Black Cavalry, or Knights of the White Camellia, took part in such a statewide spree of night riding, rowdyism, "jail deliveries," and murder that one historian, deeming them all birds of a feather, concluded that Alabama was the "most Klan-ridden state" in the South in 1869 and 1870.[35]

The Klan and its imitators were not unopposed on the field of violence. While white Republican "Mossybacks" engaged Klansmen in pitched battles in northern counties, bands of Federal soldiers, many of them rowdy and undisciplined, roved the Black Belt. Freedmen, organized by Radical Republicans into the Loyal League, were rumored to be arming themselves for sinister forays. Violence, as another historian has noted, was literally "an instrument of policy" in Reconstruction Alabama.[36]

An agent of the Justice Department assigned to anarchic Alabama during Reconstruction sent back word that "he had rather be in the heart of Comanche country than in Sumter County without soldiers."[37] Klansmen in "bloody Sumter," reputedly led by notorious former Sheriff Stephen S. Renfroe, conducted a sustained reign of terror, whipping blacks in daylight and murdering, along with several blacks, a white lawyer from New York who had been politically active among black voters.

In neighboring Greene County six blacks were murdered within a few months and the white Republican county solicitor

35. Trelease, *White Terror,* pp. 246–250.
36. Granade, "Violence," pp. 181–202.
37. Granade, "Violence," p. 199.

was dragged from his bed in Eutaw by masked men and shot to death. The murdering of white men, including a Canadian schoolteacher lynched alongside four blacks in Calhoun County in 1870, provoked the wrath of Radical Reconstructionists. Congress dispatched an investigating committee to Alabama in the summer of 1871, its Republican members hoping to tar Democrats with the Klan brush and its Democratic minority seeking to prove Radical misrule.

But as Democrats gradually regained political control, thoughtful Alabamians began to deplore regulator government. Its services no longer needed, the Klan faded from the scene, not to ride roughshod across Alabama again until the 1920s, when blacks would be only one of the minorities to experience intimidation and the lash.

In the face of this Democratic resurgence, a black man in Choctaw County mounted a challenge which briefly made his name a byword for political unrest throughout the state. Born a slave, Jack Turner became a landowner and Republican leader whose bold demands for constitutional rights attracted a large black following. County officials harassed Turner by arresting him on petty charges but Democrats did not become seriously alarmed until Choctaw went Republican in the gubernatorial campaign of August 1882. With a congressional election soon to follow, Democrats set about putting an end to Jack Turner's political activism.

Word spread through Choctaw that a mysterious packet of papers found on a public road revealed that Turner and his followers planned to massacre every white in the county. Turner and six cohorts were swiftly arrested and jailed at Butler. On a sultry August night a mob of a thousand or more whites staged a mock trial, proclaimed Jack Turner an incorrigible enemy of their race, dragged him from his cell, and hanged him from an oak tree in front of the courthouse.

The lynching of Jack Turner brought cries from Alabama Republicans and northern editors that Democrats had resorted to political murder to terrorize blacks away from the polls. (Turner's biographers attest that these suspicions were correct. They state that the papers were forged and "no such plot ever existed.'' [38]) Democrats retorted indignantly that Yankee editors were as usual pillorying Alabama and the South. In their zeal to justify the hanging of Turner, Democrats conjured up black conspiracies in virtually every congressional district in the state.

Voters in the Second District were warned against "Little John" White, a black man rumored to be inciting members of his race to stop work and kill whites. In the Third District it was whispered that a black teacher was preaching insurrection; in the Fifth District a black man was arrested on a variety of charges including urging black women not to wash clothes for white people for less than a dollar a day. In the Seventh District a former circus handyman, known as "Red Man" for his bizarre outfit of a red skull cap, red pants, and a yellow gown decorated with crosses, was arrested on a charge of exhorting blacks to violence and anarchy.

By election day in November 1882, Alabama was rife with rumors of black conspiracies. Many journalists were skeptical but few admitted their doubt publicly, leaving readers to believe that their physical safety depended upon a Democratic victory. Frightened whites hurried to the polls, many intimidated blacks stayed home, and Democrats swept every district by substantial margins. "Crying nigger" had proven effective. But Turner's biographers suggest that Democrats, in popularizing the expression "Jack Turnerism" to describe real or imaginary black protests, had unintentionally complimented a courageous man.

As Jack Turner became a symbol of political unrest, another black rebel in south Alabama was carving his niche in legendry of a different sort. Morris Slater, once a "woods-rider" who bled trees for resin on slash pine plantations and manufactured turpentine in crude stills, had taken up train robbery after he killed a deputy sheriff and fled the law. Slater broke into boxcars to steal food, axes, shotgun shells, and other goods which he sold or donated to poor blacks. He earned the nickname,

---

38. William Warren Rogers and Robert David Ward, " 'Jack Turnerism': A Political Phenomenon of the Deep South," *Journal of Negro History* 57 (October 1972): 313–332. For a fuller treatment of Jack Turner, see Rogers and Ward, *August Reckoning: Jack Turner and Racism in Post-Civil War Alabama* (Baton Rouge: Louisiana State University Press, 1973).

"Railroad Bill" and a reputation for mystic powers which enabled him to transform himself into a rabbit, opossum, or other animal to evade his pursuers.

Railroad Bill once terrorized the entire crew and passengers of a night train between Flomaton and Montgomery with only the aid of a flock of scarecrows, each holding a lantern or torch. Again he held up a train as it crossed a trestle high above the Little Escambia River, then escaped on a raft hidden beneath the bridge. But after he had killed two more sheriffs, Railroad Bill met his inevitable fate at the hands of gunmen in Atmore. Curious citizens paid twenty-five cents for a glimpse of his body when it was exhibited in every "colored" waiting room along the Louisville and Nashville Railroad line from Atmore to Greenville.

In the flatlands and red hills of south Alabama Railroad Bill became a folk hero to his people. Folklorists suggest that classic social outlaws like Robin Hood, Jesse James, or Railroad Bill, who steal from the rich and give to the poor, usually emerge during stressful times to revolt against their oppressors. Railroad Bill's popularity reflected the racial tensions of south Alabama. As the poor of England had rejoiced when Robin Hood was victorious over the Sheriff of Nottingham, poor Alabama blacks delighted in Railroad Bill's cleverness at outsmarting the white man and his law.

Although they may have viewed Railroad Bill in his coffin, many poor blacks clung to the superstition that their benefactor would return. When food was distributed to hungry people during the Great Depression, some of his old followers insisted that it had come from Railroad Bill. But their hero lived only in balladry:

> Railroad Bill was a mighty bad man
> Shot the light out the brakeman's hand
>
> *Chorus:* O ride, ride, ride
>
> Railroad Bill was a mighty spo't
> Shot all the buttons off the sheriff's coat
>
> *Chorus:* They lookin' for that bad Railroad Bill

Railroad Bill say, before he died,
He would build a railroad for the bums to ride

Chorus: Ride on, Railroad Bill.[39]

Railroad Bill, gunned down as he had slain others, and Jack Turner, hanged in front of the seat of law and order in Choctaw County, were only two of hundreds of blacks to meet violent and extralegal death in Alabama from the post-Civil War era to the onset of World War II. In the course of their political rivalries during the 1890s, Populists, Jeffersonians, Silverite and Goldbug Democrats, Black-and-Tan and Lily-White Republicans heated the smoldering embers of racism. Race relations deteriorated and the incidence of lynching rose sharply.

Tuskegee Institute, the National Association for the Advancement of Colored People, and other groups which kept the grisly record of lynchings in the United States estimate Alabama's toll between 1889 and 1940 at 303. The NAACP statistics, covering the period 1889–1918, are particularly explicit. Of 271 victims in Alabama, 237 were black; ten of these women. Murder and rape led the list of excuses for lynching, followed by robbery and arson. In addition to 71 lynchings attributed to rape, others had sexual connotations. "Paying attention to a white girl," "elopement with a white girl," and "miscegenation" appear in the statistics alongside such rationales as "poisoning mules" and "mistaken for another." [40]

Rape of white women remained the deadliest sin of which a black man could be accused. But by the 1930s moderate southerners had begun to decry lynching as an ugly scar upon their

39. Alan Lomax, *The Folk Songs of North America in the English Language* (Garden City: Doubleday and Company, 1960), pp. 557, 568–569. See also Margaret Gillis Figh, "Some Alabama Folktales," *Alabama Review* 16 (October 1963): 275. Used with permission of Alan Lomax.

40. National Association for the Advancement of Colored People, *Thirty Years of Lynching in the United States: 1889–1918* (New York: Arno Press and *New York Times,* 1969): 43–47; Southern Commission on the Study of Lynching, *Lynchings and What They Mean* (Atlanta: Southern Commission on Study of Lynching, 1931); and Jessie Daniel Ames, *The Changing Character of Lynching* (Atlanta: Commission on Interracial Cooperation, Inc., 1942).

land. Vigilantism gave way to an outward show of lawfulness with the understanding that, if rape were the charge, trial would be quick and the penalty supreme. This was the prevailing mood in Alabama during the desolate spring of 1931 when nine black youths were charged with raping two white women aboard a freight train as it traversed northern Alabama. Their case, which was not to end for almost twenty years, contained volatile ingredients (alleged rape, "niggers," Southern Womanhood, Communist agitators, and the ever-alert Yankee critics) bound to excite the old blood lust.

The first hasty trial took place amid a sullen crowd in Scottsboro. Poor-white farmers in faded overalls and women with babies on their hips jostled for seats in the courtroom or surged about the square awaiting what to them was the only conceivable verdict. These hill folk, most of them illiterate, illnourished, and impoverished, possessed little of value save their white skin. Those able to read might well have agreed with the character in an Irvin Cobb story who believed that a black rapist, hanged and burned by a mob, "got off awful light." But the people of Jackson County, restrained by state troopers, managed to "snub Judge Lynch." [41]

Eight of the nine defendants (the ninth was thirteen years old) were quickly convicted and sentenced to death. The Alabama Supreme Court affirmed seven of these convictions (the eighth was also a juvenile) but the United States Supreme Court overruled this verdict on the ground that the defendants' right to counsel had been infringed. (The high court reversed a later Scottsboro conviction because blacks had been excluded from the juries.) Tried and retried during the 1930s, the Scottsboro Case became an international *cause célèbre* as had the Sacco-Vanzetti trial during the 1920s. Communists seized upon it for propaganda purposes and many northerners joined them in pointing the finger of scorn at southern justice.

When Haywood Patterson, who had emerged as the natural leader of the defendants, was tried in Decatur, one of the women recanted her testimony and swore that no rape had taken

41. Carter, *Scottsboro,* pp. 7, 105.

place. But the remaining accuser stuck firmly by her original account. Alabama jurors could not bring themselves to take the word of black males against that of a white female on the sacrosanct question of rape. Nor were they to be swayed by the arguments of a New York lawyer (the famed Samuel Leibowitz), who had been retained by Communists, over those of their own state attorney general. When the jury demanded the death sentence, a courageous judge, James Edwin Horton, Jr., granted a new trial, setting aside the verdict as against the weight of evidence. His constituents were quick to punish Horton, rejecting him the following year for re-election.

Eventually four of the youths were convicted, one of them sentenced to death and the others to prison terms of 75 to 99 years. A fifth who pled guilty to knifing a deputy sheriff was sentenced to twenty years. Charges against four others were dropped. Judged on the same evidence, half of the "Scottsboro Boys" had been found guilty and half innocent, a paradox which satisfied neither their accusers nor their defenders and inspired the wry comment that Alabama was providing "only 50 per cent protection for the 'flower of Southern womanhood.' " [42]

Alarmed at the spreading notoriety of their state, a number of prominent white Alabamians, among them business leaders, editors, educators, and ministers, had secretly joined in an effort to ensure that the trials would be conducted fairly. Some of these, along with a national citizens' group, appealed to Gov. Bibb Graves to pardon the prisoners. The governor commuted the one death sentence to life imprisonment but, despite a personal plea from President Franklin D. Roosevelt, Graves shied away from further action, fearing that for him as for Judge Horton this would be political suicide.

While the nation was preoccupied with World War II, the Alabama Pardon and Parole Board began a quiet process of paroling the Scottsboro prisoners. Patterson, unwilling to wait for parole, escaped in 1948 and fled to Michigan, where the governor refused to extradite him. In 1950, almost twenty years

42. Carter, *Scottsboro,* p. 376.

after the nine youths had been taken from the freight train, the last defendant walked out of Kilby Prison a free man. The Scottsboro Case was closed but new entries were about to be written in the long, violence-stained ledger of race relations in Alabama.

Buttressed by Yankee soldiers during Reconstruction, black men in Alabama had briefly enjoyed the rights to vote and hold office. Even after the troops left, most freedmen remained loyal to the party of their liberation although white Republicans obstinately refused to share the spoils of power with black members. By 1890 this issue had severed Alabama Republicanism into "black-and-tans" who demanded a share of political jobs and "lily-whites" who attempted to shed the black embarrassment.

Democrats however had increasing reason to court black voters. As Alabama began to exploit its industrial potential, population drifted out of sleepy old power seats in the agrarian south to the mills and mines of the hill country, an exodus which threatened the traditional hold of Black Belt Bourbons upon legislative reins, the statehouse, and prestigious outposts in Washington. South Alabama counties needed their black majorities not merely to plant and chop cotton but to yield a harvest of votes and help justify an undue number of seats in the legislature.

By bribery, threats, and dirty tricks (such as resurrecting "dead dogs and dead niggers"), Democrats managed time and again to ensure ten thousand to thirty thousand black votes to help the party of white supremacy prevail over Republicans, Greenbackers, Jeffersonians, and Populists. Realistic Alabama politicians reconciled themselves to the fact that the "Black Belt art" of electoral fraud had "piloted the old Democratic ship from amongst the breakers on divers occasions." [43] Reuben Kolb, frustrated in his efforts to win the governorship for Populism, cried out in vain against the "Fraudocrats." [44]

43. McMillan, *Constitutional Development in Alabama*, p. 284.
44. Hackney, *Populism to Progressivism*, p. 49.

Although they had buried Populism under a black avalanche, the dawn of a new century found Alabama Democrats ready to follow the example of neighboring states in expunging black men from the voting rolls. Their motives were complex. The manipulation of tens of thousands of voters was increasingly burdensome in guilt, money, and organization. There was always a possibility, albeit dim, that black voters might escape their control and dominate the region. Explaining why his fellow Black Belt Democrats were tired of controlling black votes, one white man said: "They don't love to soil their clothes. They want the black cloud lifted somehow, any way, but surely and finally." [45]

Democrats also feared that "ignorant and vicious" whites might rekindle their Populist ardor in some other guise. To do away with their black pawns without at the same time weakening the poor-white electorate would mean political disaster. All things considered, would it not be prudent to strip the franchise from the lower white element as well as from all blacks and leave the privilege of voting to "intelligent and virtuous" whites who could be trusted to keep close guard over the bastions of property?

"Lily-white" Republicans, anxious to become politically respectable by shedding the old carpetbag-scalawag stigma, concurred. Many old Populists, although smelling a rat in disfranchisement, eventually went along in hope of removing the tool so often used to defeat them. Rallying to the battle cry of "honest elections," white men put aside political rivalries and prepared to undo much of the verdict of civil war.

Alabama's two major black leaders, rivals for stewardship of their race and legislative favors, cautioned that it would be useless and dangerous to protest. Appalled by the lynchings of the 1890s, William H. Councill, president of Alabama A. and M. College near Huntsville, had warned blacks on Emancipation Day in 1901 to guard the social barriers which separated them from their white neighbors: "The moment they become slack, the white man becomes brutal—the Negro goes down for-

45. Hackney, *Populism to Progressivism*, p. 177.

ever." [46] He advised his students to stick to their industrial studies and avoid political activism.

Booker T. Washington, foreseeing the inevitability of disfranchisement, concentrated on defeating a proposal that state funds be assigned to white and black school systems according to the share of taxes paid by each race. In the belief that educated and propertied blacks would be allowed to vote and that the illiterate and propertyless of both races would be disfranchised, Washington and thirteen black bankers, doctors, and politicians petitioned the Alabama Constitutional Convention of 1901 to give middle-class blacks "some humble share in choosing those who rule over [them]." [47] The Reverend A. F. Owens, a Mobile educator and minister, Dr. Willis E. Steers, a north Alabama physician, and William H. T. Holtzclaw, a school principal and political leader in the Black Belt, submitted individual petitions. But all were laid aside and forgotten.

Other blacks did not accept disfranchisement so pragmatically. A black newspaper scorned Booker T. Washington's petition as a prayer offered by beggars. H. V. Cashin of Huntsville warned that disfranchisement would perpetuate ring rule. Blacks at a meeting in Birmingham threatened to migrate to other states; those who gathered for a statewide rally in Camp Hill proposed a return to Africa, and another group in Colbert County petitioned Theodore Roosevelt to set aside a reservation where they might enjoy full rights of citizenship. Although no black was permitted to sit as a delegate at the constitutional convention, blacks crowded the gallery to hear the debate over their suffrage.

On the floor of the convention, whites struggled to reconcile their own differences. Uneducated and propertyless whites must be cajoled into voting for a new constitution which would eventually bar thousands like them from the political process. To ensure the co-operation of the hill counties, Black Belt Democrats must be persuaded to grant all whites temporary access to the ballot. Black voters must be eliminated by means which would

46. Hackney, *Populism to Progressivism*, p. 185.
47. Brittain, "Negro Suffrage and Politics," p. 132.

not be ruled unconstitutional in federal court. The process of resolving these issues was so tortuous that Tom Heflin proposed to hide it from view by keeping no public record of the proceedings: "We will say things down here in our Southern way that we do not want read and criticized. . . ." [48]

When the sultry summer of 1901 drew to its close, whites had written a suffrage article which, save for religion, "contained almost every qualification for voting ever devised by the mind of man" [49]—an annual, cumulative poll tax; employment; long residence in state, county, and ward; ownership of property; literacy; ability to "understand" political documents; a spotless record free from taint of vagrancy or petty crime; and, as a final barrier, powerful boards of registrars with broad discretion as to granting franchise.

Whites unable to meet the qualifications for literacy and property were appeased by the "fighting grandfather" clause which, for a few months, would admit to suffrage those men who had fought in various wars or were descended from veterans. (Some opponents warned that this might cause mulattoes to claim their white fathers and grandfathers.) Lacking a fighting grandfather or a war record, a poor-white might still achieve voting status by reason of "good character," a loophole which, one delegate jested, would admit Jesus and his Disciples only if they planned to vote Democratic. [50]

To assure their own disfranchisement, masses of blacks were manipulated one final time. Twelve Black Belt counties with more than two-thirds black population voted 36,224 to 5,741 in favor of the new constitution. Dallas, Hale, and Wilcox accounted for considerably more than half of the majority needed for ratification. The hubbub over Booker T. Washington's dinner at the White House proved an unexpected boon to those seeking to justify the new voting restrictions. "Roosevelt," rationalized the *Lafayette Sun*, "has planted more cussedness in

48. McMillan, *Constitutional Development in Alabama*, p. 270.
49. McMillan, *Constitutional Development in Alabama*, p. 359.
50. Hackney, *Populism to Progressivism*, p. 206.

the [black] race than can be gotten out except by disfranchise-ment." [51]

Despite protests from old pockets of Unionism and Populism in the hill country and wiregrass, the constitution of 1901 was adopted. The authors of its suffrage provisions, taking care not to bar blacks on the unconstitutional basis of race, set up social and economic conditions which they believed that most blacks could not meet—literacy, property, taxpaying, long-established residence, absence of petty crime. Eventually these barriers, especially the poll tax, would disfranchise more whites than blacks. Halted at the same barricades, the poor and ignorant of both races lost the essential right of citizenship.

As a sop to white sensibilities, Alabama Democrats adopted in 1902 the direct primary system of nominating party candi-dates, implying that white men would select Democratic leaders now that Populism was dead, Republicanism impotent, and blacks banished from political life. But a prophetic black editor in 1900 had foreseen the real outcome: "It is good-bye with poor white folks and niggers now." [52]

Unwilling to concede defeat, H. N. Johnson, a Mobile editor, organized the Colored Man's Suffrage Association, hired a black lawyer from New York, and brought suit.[53] The plaintiffs were Jackson William Giles, a janitor in Montgomery who had voted for twenty years, and five thousand other blacks denied suffrage because they could not answer such purposely abstruse questions as: "What are the differences between Jeffersonian Democracy and the Calhoun principles as applied to the Monroe Doctrine?" [54]

Turned aside by the Supreme Court and advised to seek help elsewhere, the association asked Congress to punish Alabama by cutting its representation in the House. But this appeal, too,

51. McMillan, *Constitutional Development in Alabama*, p. 344.

52. Hackney, *Populism to Progressivism*, p. 179.

53. For the case of Giles v. Harris (189 U.S. 475), see Loren Miller, *The Petitioners: The Story of the Supreme Court of The United States and the Negro* (Cleveland and New York: The World Publishing Company, Meridian Books, 1967), pp. 159–162.

54. Brittain, "Negro Suffrage and Politics," p. 164.

went unheeded. Several men involved in *Giles* v. *Harris* were fired from their jobs. The Suffrage Association, its members intimidated and its funds exhausted, went out of existence.

However, Peter Crenshaw, who had filed an individual suit, became the first black in Alabama granted the right to vote by court order. Others qualified under the grandfather clause, not on the basis of white ancestry but because they had served in the Civil War, the Spanish-American War, or in the Philippines. In 1902 a few blacks dared run for office. H. C. Binford and Daniel Brandon, who sought aldermen's seats in Huntsville, and Dr. George H. Wilkerson, who ran for Congress from Birmingham, even received a few white votes. But Crenshaw and the war veterans were rare exceptions. In 1900 one hundred thousand black men had been enrolled as voters in Alabama. Ten years later all but 3,752 had been "cleansed" from the voting rolls. As Democrats had hoped, the "black cloud" was lifted.

Scolded by Theodore Roosevelt for excluding blacks, Alabama Republicans made a few overtures to the remaining black voters but "lily-whites" eventually gained firm control of their party. In 1904 some black voters even turned to the party of white supremacy, heeding the advice of one of their editors that it was better to vote "for an avowed enemy . . . than for a false friend." [55] But the great majority of Alabama blacks slumped into political apathy. By the early 1930s only 1,500 to 1,800 remained on the voting rolls; even ballots cast by such obviously qualified blacks as Dr. Robert R. Moton, principal of Tuskegee Institute, and Dr. H. C. Trenholm, president of Alabama State University, were challenged.

In 1944 the Supreme Court forbade the Democratic party to exclude any person from its primaries on the basis of race. Fearing a massive black influx to formerly all-white primaries (winning the Democratic primary was equivalent to election), Alabama whites threw up a hasty new barricade. The Boswell amendment required that a prospective voter not only be able to read and write any article of the United States Constitution

55. Brittain, "Negro Suffrage and Politics," p. 161.

but—a crucial step—"understand" it to the satisfaction of a local board of registrars. After all, an author of the amendment cautioned, "a small parrot could be taught to recite a section of our Constitution." [56]

Despite the supplications of blacks who set aside a Sunday to pray for its defeat, the Boswell amendment was approved by Alabama voters in 1946. Although urged to reject the amendment by James E. Folsom, the popular governor-nominee, by Senator Lister Hill, and by senator-nominee John Sparkman, most white voters had responded once again to the old emotional rhetoric of racism. The amendment, challenged in federal court by ten black leaders from Mobile, was ruled unconstitutional by the Supreme Court in 1949.[57]

White politicians, however, had limitless cunning. In 1951 a voter qualification amendment authorized the Alabama Supreme Court to prepare a questionnaire to guide registrars in deciding which prospective voters could "understand" the documents of citizenship. Governor Folsom, imprudently for his political future, protested "too many [blacks] have maliciously been denied the right to vote . . . that is not democracy in any sense." [58] Half a century after their disfranchisement, only 5 percent of blacks over the age of twenty-one in Alabama managed to exercise the right to vote. No other state (not even Mississippi) still guarded the Bastille of white supremacy so jealously.

The walls of segregation in Alabama did not come tumbling down, like those of Jericho, after one mighty blast of trumpets. Blacks were to achieve this victory one step at a time, every attack met by counterattack to the very eve of surrender. No inch of ground would be conceded and no battlement fall without bitter contest. There would be street fighting in Montgomery, Birmingham, Anniston, Selma, and Tuscaloosa; verbal battles in

56. Barnard, *Dixiecrats and Democrats,* p. 61.

57. For the case of Davis v. Schnell (336 U.S. 933), see Miller, *The Petitioners,* p. 301.

58. Brittain, "Negro Suffrage and Politics," p. 186.

Congress, the Supreme Court, and the White House. Forty
years after the death of Booker T. Washington, Martin Luther
King, Jr., would be tested in the crucible of Alabama and
emerge as the new leader of the black masses.

Having met with failure in the courts, a few blacks turned to
street demonstrations as early as 1926. Indiana Little, a schoolteacher, led a thousand Birmingham protesters that year in a
march to dramatize the fact that only five hundred blacks in the
most populous county in Alabama were permitted to vote. Black
veterans of the war "to save the world for democracy" also appealed in vain for the privilege of voting in their native state. In
1937, perhaps emboldened by worldwide displays of sympathy
for the Scottsboro defendants, blacks again took to the streets of
Birmingham, singing (to the tune of "Battle Hymn of the Republic") of a dream which would not be realized for thirty
years:

> Negroes voting with the whites
> Will put across the Bill of Rights.
> Jim Crow voting now is dead
> Gonna have Democracy instead.
> Gonna Register! [59]

From the beginning black women took their places alongside
men in the ranks of protesters. More women than men marched
with Indiana Little, only to see their leader arrested for vagrancy
and their appeal ignored. But thirty years later, when Rosa
Parks refused to yield her seat in a crowded Montgomery bus to
a white man, she inspired the first display of the effectiveness of
massive, nonviolent resistance in the civil rights struggle. Aure-
lia S. Browder, who challenged bus segregation in the courts,
was also victorious. In 1956 her case came before a Supreme
Court with a concept of duty far beyond that held by the Court
which had turned aside the plea of the Colored Man's Suffrage
Association. Affirming a lower court decision, the Supreme
Court agreed with Circuit Court Judge Richard Rives that
Montgomery ordinances and Alabama statutes requiring racial

---

59. Brittain, "Negro Suffrage and Politics," pp. 177–179.

segregation on municipal transit lines violated the due process and equal protection clauses of the Fourteenth Amendment. In the area of state and local transportation, the high court had, by implication, overruled the "separate but equal" formula announced in *Plessy* v. *Ferguson* sixty years earlier.[60]

Another Alabama black woman, too proud to tolerate servility, won a little-noticed legal victory in 1964. To some the issue may have appeared trivial but Mary Hamilton felt strongly about it and the Supreme Court deemed it worthy of hearing. Mary Hamilton had refused to answer on a witness stand when an attorney called her "Mary." The high court assured her that, in courtrooms of Alabama henceforth, she and others of her race were entitled to be addressed with the same respect accorded to whites.[61]

Autherine Lucy, Vivian Malone, and James A. Hood braved insults and danger to help break down the barriers against black students at the University of Alabama in Tuscaloosa. Eventually blacks and whites by the thousands would sit together in the colleges and public schools of Alabama. Black children no longer feel bewildered or angry, as Coretta Scott once felt, because they are consigned to separate schools. Coretta Scott was one of the fortunate few to escape from the educational malnutrition suffered by most black children in Alabama in the 1930s. She attended Antioch College in Ohio and the New England Conservatory in Boston, where she met and married Martin Luther King, Jr. But she never forgot that she had walked three miles each day to a "colored" school near Marion while buses filled with white children passed her, raising dust or spattering mud. "I remember resenting that," she wrote years later.[62]

Coretta Scott King would be proud to walk up Dexter Avenue in 1965 at the side of her husband to climax the momentous

60. For the case of Gayle v. Browder (352 U.S. 903), see Miller, *The Petitioners,* p. 283.

61. For the case of Hamilton v. Alabama (376 U.S. 61), see Miller, *The Petitioners,* p. 283.

62. Coretta Scott King, *My Life with Martin Luther King, Jr.* (New York: Holt, Rinehart and Winston, 1969), pp. 32–33.

march from Selma to Montgomery. Other leaders of the movement, who marched triumphantly with Dr. King that day, had deep associations and old memories of Alabama. John Lewis, the son of a tenant farmer, had spent his boyhood near Troy and had been inspired to his first protest at fifteen by the example of Rosa Parks. Ralph David Abernathy had grown up in Linden in the heart of the Black Belt. Andrew Young had married a girl from Marion and had taught one summer at nearby Lincoln Normal School, a semiprivate school for blacks founded by the American Missionary Association after the Civil War.

When the civil rights movement began to focus upon urban areas, Lewis, Abernathy, and Young elected to remain in the South. Lewis, chairman of the militant Student Non-Violent Coordinating Committee (SNCC) and one of the first to be clubbed at the Pettus Bridge in Selma on "Bloody Sunday" in 1965, became administrator of the Voter Education Project with headquarters in Atlanta. After Dr. King was assassinated, his friend Ralph David Abernathy succeeded him as leader of the Southern Christian Leadership Conference. Andrew Young became the first black to represent Atlanta in Congress.

Many Alabama blacks who pioneered in the struggle for civil rights remained in their home state to witness startling changes wrought, to some degree, by their own efforts. Arthur D. Shores, denied permission to run for public office in 1942, became the first black to sit on the Birmingham City Council. Other early leaders saw the racial mores of their communities undergo major transformation: among them, Emory Jackson, E. Paul Jones, Peter Hall, Edward Gardner, and W. C. Patton in Birmingham; E. D. Nixon, Rufus A. Lewis, and James E. Price in Montgomery; C. G. Gomillion and William P. Mitchell in Tuskegee; Amelia Platt Boynton and Frederick D. Reese in Selma, John L. LeFlore and J. J. Thomas in Mobile.

But seven young blacks did not live to see the barriers fall. Jimmy Lee Jackson, 25, shot to death by a state trooper during the demonstrations at Marion; Cynthia Wesley, 14; Carol Robertson, 14; Addie Mae Collins, 14; and Denise McNair, 11—all killed when a bomb exploded in their Sunday School classroom in Birmingham; and Virgil Wade, 13, and Johnny

Robinson, 16, fatally shot in the turmoil which followed that bombing.

Two of the thousands deeply affected by the tragedy at the Sixteenth Street Baptist Church went quite different directions after the bombing. Angela Davis, who had been a neighbor and friend of the four girls, became a college professor in California, an avowed Communist and speaker for radical causes, a fugitive and the central figure of a celebrated trial in which she was eventually acquitted. Chris McNair, the father of Denise, conquered his bitterness, worked within the system, and became the first black chairman of the Jefferson County delegation to the Alabama legislature.

In the course of many trials and tribulations, Alabama blacks have achieved far-reaching victories for themselves and for all Americans. Ruling on the Scottsboro cases, the Supreme Court served notice that it would intervene when states failed to assure due process and equal protection of the laws for criminal defendants. Those accused of capital crimes must have the services of an attorney, the Court held, and racial discrimination in the selection of juries would no longer be tolerated. [63]

C. G. Gomillion, who protested when the town of Tuskegee was gerrymandered to exclude black voters, moved the Court one step further toward its landmark decision that it could command states to reapportion their legislatures in hope of achieving the democratic concept of "one man, one vote." [64] Hundreds of anonymous Alabama blacks, accosted by firehoses and dogs in Birmingham and turned back with clubs and tear gas in Selma, helped write into the statutes of the nation the Civil Rights Act of 1964 and the Voting Rights Act of 1965.

By 1975 blacks enjoyed all public facilities in Alabama, rode in whatever seats they chose on buses and trains, attended public schools and universities, and cast their ballots freely, more than 300,000 being registered to vote. There were 161 black of-

---

63. The cases are Powell v. Alabama (287 U.S. 45), Norris v. Alabama (294 U.S. 587), and Patterson v. Alabama (294 U.S. 600).

64. The case of Gomillion v. Lightfoot (364 U.S. 339) was a forerunner of Baker v. Carr (369 U.S. 186).

ficeholders in the state, including 2 state senators, 13 members
of the state house, 17 county officials, 58 municipal officers
including 8 mayors, 40 elected law enforcement officers
including sheriffs, and 20 members of school boards. Among
the fifty states of the union, Alabama ranked eighth in number
of blacks holding elective office.

At long last the words of the old slave song could be read,
not as a hope of heavenly reward, but as a prophecy realized in
Alabama:

> My strongs' trial now is pas'
> My triumph jes' begun.[65]

65. *Alabama Narratives*, p. 210.

3

Build Thee More Stately Mansions:
The Shifting Haunts of Power

*Build thee more stately mansions, O my soul, As the swift
seasons roll!*
—"The Chambered Nautilus," Oliver Wendell Holmes

*O*LD Federal Road, following the trails of pioneers and Indian fighters, entered Alabama below present-day Phenix City,
ran the gauntlet of Creek Indian territory, threaded swollen
streams, carved a faint path through pine forests, skirted
swamps where Spanish moss hung from ancient oaks, and eventually reached Montgomery. From this rude trading post, the
trace meandered south of the Alabama River to Saint Stephens
and struck in a westerly direction toward the Mississippi.

The most important land artery in early Alabama, Federal
Road was the route by which wagonloads of ambitious and adventurous settlers struggled to reach a crescent of fertile land
known as the Black Belt which stretched from Fort Mitchell on
the Chattahoochee to Gainesville on the Tombigbee, thence into
Mississippi. This dark, chalky soil, it was rumored, would yield
cotton in such abundance as to make rich men richer, transform
farmers into planters, beget fortunes, and establish dynasties.

Propelled by such visions, Israel Pickens and his family endured six weeks on Federal Road to reach Greene County from North Carolina. The Lides of South Carolina, beset by frequent breakdowns in their wagon train and ever fearful of Indians, travelled for five weeks at the painfully slow pace of fifteen miles a day to claim 490 choice acres in Dallas County for four dollars an acre. Charles Tait migrated from Georgia to Wilcox County in 1818 with twenty-five field hands. By the time of his death in 1835 he had increased his slaveholdings to 115; his son James more than doubled this number by 1841.

Joseph Baldwin, one of the hundreds who migrated to southern Alabama in quest of fortune, was exhilarated by the contrast between a scene of feverish speculation and the staid Virginia society from which he had come. Men were rewarded in the Black Belt, not on the basis of ancestry, but in proportion to their boldness, enterprise, or skill at gambling, swindling, and cheating. "There is no stopping in such a society," young Baldwin observed. "He who does not go ahead is run over and trodden down." [1]

Most tidewater planters, content with the spoils of an earlier land rush, saw no reason to abandon fiefs in the Virginia or South Carolina lowlands for an uncertain future in Alabama. Some scions of wealthy families sought a fresh bonanza, forming small coteries of gentility around Eufaula and Cahaba. But restless farmers from the piedmont, hungry for wealth and position, made up the majority of those who trekked south on Federal Road. Like Joseph Baldwin, they thrived in a contest where no holds were barred, "where the stranger of yesterday is the man of mark today . . . where amidst a host of competitors in an open field of rivalry, every man . . . enters the course with a race-horse emulation, to win the prize which is glittering within sight of the rivals." [2]

If blessed with bountiful crops, a fortunate marriage (perhaps to a cousin whose acreage adjoined his own), and a cool head

---

1. Joseph Baldwin, *The Flush Times of Alabama and Mississippi* (New York: Hill and Wang, American Century Series, 1957), p. 167.
2. Baldwin, *Flush Times,* p. 167.

for business, a farmer might quickly acquire the means to cover
his log cabin with white clapboards, add columns, a veranda,
and a second story, and proclaim himself to the manor born.
But no matter how many professional historians like Thomas
Perkins Abernethy reasoned that only men who needed to better
their fortunes transplanted their families to a wilderness; no matter that these emigrants were characterized by W. J. Cash as
"cotton snobs," *nouveaux,* and "the natural flower of the back
country grown prosperous," [3] their claim to aristocratic
(preferably Virginia) lineage would become generally accepted.
The notion that behind every Greek portico once dwelt a blue
blood became a staple of Alabama mythology.

Civil war dealt a mortal blow to this feudal society. Planters
substituted tenantry and peonage for slavery but never recovered
from the emancipation of their labor force. Cotton culture has
been largely superseded by soybeans and cattle, yet the Big
House still enthralls Alabama. This columned mansion remains
the pre-eminent icon of the white citizenry, even of those whose
forebears built no stately houses, owned no slaves, clung to the
Union, and dared to defy the Bourbons.

What accounts for this enduring appeal in a state settled
mainly by plain farm folk? Cash postulated that former Confederate soldiers, long after Appomattox, found it hard to break
away from the habit of obedience to their haughty old colonels.
Despite a brief eruption of Populism and the siren calls of numerous demagogues, white southerners of the middle and lower
economic orders *do* retain a certain subservience to their native
aristocracy, recognizing them instinctively by their dress, their
speech, and their bearing. But the plantation mystique is based
upon more than class consciousness. Like antebellum yeomen,
many modern southerners are also upward bound; desiring some
mansion of their own choosing, they are careful not to destroy
this vision.

But above all the Big House is a romantic symbol to people
of a more mundane era. Even cynical Yankees and resolute

3. Cash, *Mind of the South,* p. 21.

iconoclasts are intrigued, returning from the Alabama lowlands with a guilty sense of having been seduced or a yearning to own an antebellum showplace. "The Black Belt," confessed Carl Carmer, "became in my mind a country apart, perhaps under an especial enchantment—exerting a softly insistent influence on all those who have ever trod its dark soil." [4] (Was Carl Carmer actually enchanted by a land now lonely, dull, and depopulated, or simply under the "softly insistent influence" of mint juleps?)

For lack of a more satisfying explanation of its remarkable durability and broad appeal, the mystique of the plantation might be attributed to a certain irony in the American nature: that average citizens and underdogs enjoy an occasional glimpse of the trappings of wealth and power, having forgotten their terrible price.

About two thousand of Alabama's antebellum mansions survived into the mid-twentieth century, scattered from the Tennessee valley to Mobile but concentrated mostly in the Black Belt. Many of these were plain country houses embellished by pillars and a veranda, barely qualifying as mansions. Roving carpenters, using a single pattern, built dozens of almost identical houses in the antebellum villages of Alabama, square or T-shaped with central halls, pinched facades, and plain posts supporting the upper and lower porches. Other planters, unable to find or to afford an architect, improvised their plans from a popular handbook which reflected the rage for Greek and Roman architecture. Thus hundreds of two-story houses, as stereotyped as units in a modern suburb, sprang up across the lowlands.

This practical but unimaginative structure was remarkably well adapted to the humid subtropics. Spacious halls, high ceilings, and tall, shuttered windows admitted any vagrant breeze of the long, sultry summer. Fireplaces to offset dampness and chill were indispensable features of every room. Builders, working under primitive conditions, made use of their own timber and instructed slaves to contrive columns, pediments, casings, mantels, and bricks from native materials. "They fashioned

---

4. Carmer, *Stars Fell on Alabama*, p. 121.

Greek Revival mansions from red clay and pine trees,'' Ralph Hammond marvelled, ''and they did it well.'' [5]

But the Grand Mansions of Alabama are relatively few. Hammond chose sixty-four to be pictured in a book as examples of grandeur or of the eccentricity of their owners, evidently considering the remainder as lesser structures or only slight variations on a theme. The ratio of Grand Mansions to garden-variety mansions roughly illustrates the ratio of super-planters to typical masters. In 1860 only about one-third of Alabama families owned slaves and one-half of these owned less than five. Among large slaveowners, the typical master owned from 50 to 100 slaves; only twenty-four planters owned 200 to 300; only ten owned from 300 to 500; a few were rumored to own as many as 1,000. Charles and James Tait, who so multiplied their slaveholdings, were the exception rather than the rule.

The most prosperous planters garnished their original homes with iron grillwork, frescoes, marble mantels, and spiral staircases or built finer houses, perhaps topped with cupolas and equipped with ballrooms. Onetime farmers acquired a taste for elegance by marrying into the ranks of patricians or observing their adornments. Some mansions were ornamented with silver doorknobs, solid walnut stairways, crystal chandeliers, ruby or stained glass transoms, ceilings edged in gold leaf, and marble-floored entries. Furnishings were comparable: Brussels or Oriental carpets, damask drapes, and gilt-edged mirrors; massive poster beds, banquet tables, and sideboards of mahogany, walnut, or rosewood; numerous life-sized portraits.

But it is the exterior rather than the interior of the mansion which is stamped indelibly upon the American psyche. Its appearance from afar, pale and shimmering on some rural acropolis or looming at the end of a lane of trees, contributes to its impact. One awestruck visitor, approaching a Barbour County mansion down a long alley of water oaks, felt ''as if I were entering a church.'' [6] Its whiteness is also part of the mystique

5. Ralph Hammond, *Ante-Bellum Mansions of Alabama* (New York: Crown Publishers, Bonanza Books, 1951), p. 29.

6. Walker, *Backtracking in Barbour County,* pp. 134–162.

even though archivists insist that Gaineswood was originally ocher and that other mansions were painted in pastel shades.

To enhance their effect as well as for practical reasons, mansions were located atop knolls, on bluffs overlooking the river, or at the forks of creeks. Their names reflect these surroundings but, as Carl Carmer noted, also betray a taste for the poetic on the part of acquisitive planters (Rosemount, Thornhill, Magnolia Grove, Bluff Hall, Alpine, Forks of Cypress). One great house was christened Pitts Folly by those who scoffed while its builder, Philip Henry Pitts, raised his ambitious structure near Uniontown in the prosperous 1850s. But Pitts Folly pales in comparison with Gaineswood, its pretentious neighbor in Demopolis, created by an imaginative builder-owner, Gen. Nathan Bryan Whitfield, who tinkered with his grand house for twenty years, adding porticos, domes, and pavilions as the whim struck him and shamelessly mixing Greek Revival, Renaissance Revival, and Italianate styles.

But columns are essential to the aura of a southern mansion; remove them and only a large box remains. The Forks of Cypress near Florence was surrounded by twenty-four massive columns fashioned from blocks of wood overlaid with a stucco of horsehair, charcoal, sand, and molasses. Although the central structure burned, all but one of these columns still stand, defiant of fire and time. Each of the six great Doric columns of Belle Mina near Huntsville is believed to have been made of a single poplar tree, covered with brick and plaster; those of Pitts Folly are solid walnut. The architect who designed the President's Mansion at the University of Alabama in Tuscaloosa elevated the low country "raised cottage" motif to grandeur by six Ionic columns, and a neoclassical facade. Sturdivant Hall in Selma is one of the relatively few Alabama mansions to exhibit Corinthian columns. Old Homestead in Lowndesboro has immense columns in keeping with the dimensions of Dixon Hall Lewis, who weighed five hundred pounds and believed that the house should reflect the man. If fronted only by a row of white wooden columns, the plainest country house gives off an air of importance and authority.

Perhaps this aura also derives from the fact that these houses were planned by men rather than women. Forks of Cypress, Ralph Hammond said, was "definitely a man's house," its exterior suggesting "boldness and masculinity." [7] Philip Henry Pitts used the first person singular when he wrote in his diary: "On Friday, February 27, 1852, I commenced raising my new house in Uniontown." [8]

These builders evinced concern for the most minute details of pediment, medallion, or banister. General Whitfield sent to Paris for two floor-to-ceiling mirrors, to be placed in such precise relation to one another that visitors could see his drawing room reflected thirteen times. Col. Edward Watts insisted that Sturdivant Hall, like other great mansions, should have its spiral stairway but Robert Watkins, Jr., was not content until his Huntsville home had three such stairways. Walker Reynolds journeyed to New York (taking along his wife, Hannah) to choose the fine furnishings of Mount Ida.

What do their homes tell of the nature of these Alabama planters? Certainly the most baronial houses betray their owners as among America's conspicuous consumers, free from Puritan scruples about showiness and lavish expenditure even when heavily in debt. They imported fieldstone from England and mantels of carved Carrara marble from Italy, brought artisans from Virginia to execute plasterwork and stairways, summoned a gardener from Ireland or a landscapist from France to arrange boxwoods in the shape of a lyre. John McNab rode about Eufaula in his silver-mounted carriage when he was not abroad buying up bolts of Irish linen, Scotch tweed, and rare laces; numerous silk shawls; and enough Chinese tea to last until the next journey.

Their mansions bespeak a sociable nature and a yearning for entertainment to allay the loneliness and fears of backwoods existence. Some planters built in neighborly clusters as at Lowndesboro, Dayton, Gainesville, and Cahaba, travelling to their fields each day. Reception rooms, double parlors, large dining rooms, and ballrooms indicate that houses were planned

---

7. Hammond, *Ante-Bellum Mansions,* p. 33.
8. Hammond, *Ante-Bellum Mansions,* p. 138.

with hospitality in mind. Seventy-five to one hundred guests could be served comfortably in the dining room of the E. M. Perine mansion at Cahaba. Dances at Rosemount took place in a great hall extending sixty feet across the house. Indians are said to have peered into the windows of the Gaineswood ballroom to marvel at the Virginia reel and minuet. Robert Jemison maintained a billiard room and gameroom in the cellar of his mansion Cherokee in Tuscaloosa. Wine cellars, smokehouses, and commodious kitchens attest to the importance of food and drink in every mansion.

Although equipped with facilities for sumptuous entertaining, Alabama planters seldom dedicated an entire room to such a contemplative pursuit as reading. Thomas Bibb appears to have been an unusual mansion builder in that he included a library at Belle Mina and in the mansion he built for his daughter in Huntsville. Not even Gaineswood had a separate room designated as a library. This is not to claim that antebellum gentry did not read, only that they evidently gave entertainment a higher priority in terms of space. Many planters exhorted their sons to read Greek and Roman classics like Plutarch's *Lives* so they would be imbued with sagas of heroic men, familiar with the cadences of Cicero's oratory, and bolstered by the glory of slave societies. For lighter reading they were encouraged to peruse the novels of Sir Walter Scott, whose picturization of English nobility served them as a model, and stories and poems by that fellow southern romantic, Edgar Allan Poe.

The concept of planters as men who favored action over contemplation and were determined to prevail over all obstacles is reflected in legends which surround their houses. Allen Glover, refusing to postpone his daughter's wedding although Demopolis was isolated by floods, ordered a hundred slaves to stand on stumps holding torches so that a nervous minister could see his way across the swirling waters. After a nightlong struggle, Glover and his torchbearers triumphantly escorted the rector into the presence of bride, groom, and guests. General Whitfield, annoyed that his ballroom was not complete in time for a family wedding, demanded that the unfinished wall be covered by a huge canvas painted with cornices, mirrors, and columns. (Evidently his guests were well supplied with champagne; few noticed the illusion.) James Jackson delighted in displaying his champion racehorses on a full-sized track on the front lawn of Forks of Cypress.

Visitors to antebellum Alabama offered other clues to the nature of planters. Frederick Olmsted found them bold and self-reliant, "under a little alcoholic excitement" much of the time, but shallow and purely objective in expressing ideas.[9] The English actor Tyrone Power pronounced Montgomery planters "a merry set of fellows, and many of them exceedingly intelligent."[10] But Capt. Basil Hall, a British naval officer who booked passage on an Alabama River steamer in 1827, thought his fellow passengers tiresome because they talked of only one subject, the price of cotton.

Philip Gosse, an English tutor, described the sons of Dallas County planters as more adept at hunting rabbits than conjugating verbs, more skilled in wilderness lore than concerned with written knowledge or city ways. He also found it prudent to keep his opinion about the institution of slavery to himself, betraying no sympathy for slaves nor curiosity about their treatment. "There is a very stern jealousy of a stranger's interference on these points," he noted in a letter home.[11] Being from England, Gosse might be an acceptable schoolmaster, provided he held his tongue, but Alabama planters of the 1850s kept vigilant watch lest abolitionists slip into their midst in the guise of educators. Advertising for a teacher in 1859 a Camden schoolmaster put it bluntly: "No Yankees need apply."[12]

Indeed why read if dangerous thoughts lurked in magazines, books, and the minds of teachers? During the decade of the fifties, planters were exhorted to withdraw their sons from northern colleges, harden their attitude against public education and

9. Olmsted, *The Cotton Kingdom,* pp. 100–101.

10. Clanton W. Williams, "Early Ante-Bellum Montgomery: A Black Belt Constituency," *Journal of Southern History* 7 (November 1941): 512.

11. Philip Henry Gosse, *Letters from Alabama (U.S.) Chiefly Relating to Natural History* (London: Morgan and Chase, 1859), pp. 33–34.

12. Walter M. Jackson, *The Story of Selma* (Birmingham: Birmingham Printing Company, 1954): p. 189.

suppress all Yankee "isms," including intellectualism. Leave the contemplative life to northerners; southern youth had more exciting things to do. Who would choose to *read* when he could hunt, gamble, duel, dance, drill, compete in knightly tournaments, or attend cockfights, horseraces, barbecues, political rallies, and celebrations of the Fourth of July?

Planters pursued hunting as passionately as did plain folk of the hills, stalking deer, 'possum, raccoon, wild hog, squirrel, fox, turkey, partridge, and quail. Observing this southern ritual, Gosse concluded that hunting was an appropriate pastime for men who lived in the isolation of vast forests, far from city amusements: "Self-defence [*sic*] and the natural craving for excitement, compel him to be a hunter." [13]

Deer hunters lined the forest paths and shot their quarry wholesale, felling as many as seventy in a single day. Other men pursued deer by horseback, plunging recklessly through the trees, or lay in wait for them in canoes near their watering holes. Skill with the long rifle was the proudest boast of this male society. Emulating English bowmen who could split a peeled wand at a hundred paces, Alabama planters and their sons practiced patiently in attempts to hammer a nail into a post with one bullet, shoot through an auger hole without touching the plank, "snuff" a candle so briefly that it flamed anew, or aim a rifle ball into a tree so precisely that a squirrel was killed by the concussion "without a wound or ruffled hair." [14]

Pleasure, whether derived from lavish entertaining, country revels, travelling, eating, drinking, or hunting, provided planters with escape from rural tedium, fretting over the price of cotton, or supervising the daily routine of the plantation. They evinced their romantic nature by pretending to be English nobility, riding in tournaments dressed like knights, practicing marksmanship, duelling, or adorning their mansions. They reflected their actual experience on the western frontier by open hospitality to strangers, zest for hunting, and rustic pursuits like cockfighting, gambling, and barbecuing.

13. Gosse, *Letters from Alabama,* p. 130.
14. Gosse, *Letters from Alabama,* p. 133.

Long after the plantation era had ended, Carl Carmer found descendants of planters still pursuing pleasure in the 1920s, partying and hunting as fervently as ever and engaging in newer pastimes like bridge, golf, and tennis. "I reckon Alabama's about the only place left where exciting things can happen to the gentility," one boasted.[15] But an elderly professor in Tuscaloosa warned Carmer not to linger overlong in Alabama lest he lose track of the passage of time and his mind become anesthetized by pleasure-seeking.

Departing the Black Belt of a late afternoon, eager to welcome the neon of Birmingham, one can glimpse a few of the lonely mansions. Gaineswood, Sturdivant Hall, and Bluff Hall are museums now, carefully furnished but lifeless. Others have been restored and fittingly adorned with period furnishings by new owners with the means to maintain private showplaces. (Although some have been desecrated by twentieth-century *nouveaux* whose tastes run to giant television consoles, vinyl lounge chairs, and plastic dinettes.) Pitts Folly, hunched behind a cotton gin and almost obscured by a thicket of trees, is still owned by descendants of Philip Henry Pitts. Rosemount and Thornhill, silhouetted against the lingering light of a winter sunset, have changed hands often. Many Big Houses stand empty, slowly rotting in the humid air of the Black Belt, abandoned to the elements and to phantoms of the past.

What of that shadowy creature who shared the planter's four-poster? Some firsthand observers of antebellum Alabama, if judged by their writings, saw no women at all. Philip Gosse, who described virtually every species of flora and fauna in the state, made almost no mention of women. Frederick Olmsted and James Buckingham, so curious about other aspects of this society, apparently had no interest in or contact with women of the gentility. Women were invisible to some male writers of more recent vintage. Ralph Hammond had almost nothing to say of the wives of mansion builders. Jesse G. Whitfield, recollecting his childhood days at Gaineswood, expressed much admira-

15. Carmer, *Stars Fell on Alabama,* p. 9.

tion for his inventive grandfather but never mentioned his grandmother, who bore General Whitfield twelve children.

Dozens of men gambled, fought, and matched legal wits in the tales of Joseph Baldwin but women appeared merely as decorations. This young Virginian described the daughters of one planter as "good housewife girls . . . at home, abroad, on horseback, or on foot, at the piano, or discoursing on the old English books." [16] Such girls, Baldwin confessed, were so much alike that he found it difficult to decide between them. This view is echoed in an account written in 1853 by a young man who attended a party at the Presbyterian Female College in Talladega. One belle was "musically accomplished, charming, polite and amiable"; another was "so agreeable, smiling, beautiful, so profusely ringletted"; others were "amiable, intelligent, accomplished, beautiful." [17] Indeed how was a man to choose?

The search for the antebellum Southern Lady is rendered difficult by her invisibility and her subjection to stereotyping and myth. Some scholars have sought to unearth her by reading early novels about the plantation era. But they discover only two types of Southern Ladies inhabiting these fictional mansions: Ornamental Womanhood, made of flesh and blood but only slightly more useful than a piece of statuary; and Romantic Womanhood, dedicated to submission, domesticity, and her family. In whichever of these roles they appear, women are overshadowed in old novels by fathers, husbands, and sons.

Men were major influences in fashioning both the myth and the actual woman. Fathers began early the process of instructing daughters in the qualities which they deemed desirable for a woman: sweetness, charm, and, above all, dutifulness. If a daughter learned these lessons well, she might be lavishly rewarded. As a wedding gift to his daughter Thomas Bibb built a Greek Revival mansion in Huntsville which cost $32,000 even though constructed in the late 1820s with slave labor. Walker

16. Baldwin, *Flush Times,* p. 73.
17. Minnie Clare Boyd, *Alabama in the Fifties: A Social Study* (New York: AMS Press, 1966), p. 222.

Reynolds provided such a magnificent wedding gown for his daughter Maud that it won second prize in 1939 among all the old gowns entered in a contest at the premier of "Gone With the Wind." Fatherly devotion was often fervently returned. Betty-Louise Clarke Prynelle, who wrote a romanticized concept of childhood on an Alabama plantation, expressed the feeling of many a daughter in her dedication of *Diddie, Dumps and Tot:* "To my dear father, Dr. Richard Clarke, of Selma, Alabama, my hero and beau ideal of a gentleman." [18]

The more formal education of a Southern Belle took place at female academies where she studied piano, guitar, drawing, or French; or at a college like Judson in Marion, where parents were assured that daughters would be "tenderly guarded in all that is dear to a parent's heart." Any young lady so unwise as to behave in a "perverse or obstinate" fashion would be requested to withdraw. Judson desired no rebels, only those "such as are happy in observing wise and wholesome regulation." [19]

Her education completed, a belle's proper destiny was marriage. Anna M. Gayle Fry, although reared in the planter community of Cahaba, perpetuated a fictional view of the leisurely plantation mistress who spent her morning in reading, conversation, or needlework, napped midday, went visiting or driving in the afternoon, and danced until exhausted each night. "No special labor was pressing," Mrs. Fry assured her many readers.[20] She must have forgotten or been too young to notice that these women, although frequently pregnant, were engaged in the tasks of sewing, mending, supervising meals, attending to the health and Christian training of children and slaves, and entertaining an unending stream of guests.

Of all the burdens upon a plantation mistress, the heaviest was that so many people depended upon her. Such women,

18. Betty-Louise Clarke Prynelle, *Diddie, Dumps and Tot: or Plantation Child-Life* (New York: Harper and Brothers, 1882).

19. Lucille Griffith, *History of Alabama, 1540–1900: As Recorded in Diaries, Letters, and Papers of the Times* (Northport, Ala.: Colonial Press, 1962), pp. 125–126.

20. Anna M. Gayle Fry, *Memories of Old Cahaba* (Nashville: Printed for the Author, 1908), pp. 61–62.

Mary Boykin Chesnut believed, had less chance to live their own lives than missionaries to Africa. Mrs. Chesnut, although the wife of a Confederate brigadier general and the daughter of a South Carolina governor, was, like many another southern woman, a secret abolitionist. While she and her husband lived in Montgomery in 1861, Mrs. Chesnut witnessed a sight which strengthened her belief that slavery was an evil. High on the Montgomery slave block stood "a bright, mulatto woman . . . magnificently gotten up in silks and satins . . . sometimes ogling the bidders, sometimes looking quite coy and modest." To her diary Mrs. Chesnut confided her horror over this scene:

> My very soul sickened . . . I tried to reason "You know how women sell themselves and are sold in marriage, from queens downwards, eh? You know what the Bible says about slavery and marriage. Poor women, poor slaves." [21]

Auctions like this illustrated for Mrs. Chesnut the iniquity of a system which allowed men to live like patriarchs of old, surrounded by wives, concubines, and by white and mulatto children who bore a distinct resemblance to one another. "Any lady," Mrs. Chesnut wrote, "is ready to tell you who is the father of all the mulatto children in everybody's household but her own. Those, she seems to think, drop from the clouds." [22]

One of Mrs. Chesnut's contemporaries, Victoria Clayton of Eufaula, also found support in the Bible for a view which received much wider currency in the South. Slavery, she concluded, was a paternalistic responsibility to be endured and exercised with care although it required her to supervise the feeding of her slaves, sew their clothing, and oversee their prayers. Even this dedicated plantation mistress permitted herself to hint that she might have preferred it otherwise: "Many of us thought Slavery [sic] a curse to our land. Yet what were we to do but to make the best of existing laws and environments?" [23]

21. Mary Boykin Chesnut, *A Diary From Dixie*, ed. Ben Ames Williams (Boston: Houghton-Mifflin Co., 1949), pp. 10–11.

22. Chesnut, *Diary from Dixie*, pp. 21–22.

23. Victoria Virginia Clayton, *White and Black Under the Old Regime* (Freeport, N.Y.: Books for Libraries Press, 1970), pp. 51–57, 188. For an analysis, see Anne

Historians, in belated search of women's history, are beginning to peel away layers of myth to reveal real women, engaged in a herculean effort to fulfill all the roles expected of them: Gracious Hostess, Exemplary Mother, Beloved Mistress to her slaves, and Practical Helpmeet to her husband. Victoria Clayton, recalling her antebellum upbringing in Eufaula, was frank to say why she had attracted her husband-to-be: Henry D. Clayton had noted how efficiently this seventeen-year-old girl managed her father's household. "No practical man . . . ," wrote the forthright Victoria, "desires a useless woman to share with him the 'changes and chances of this mortal life.' " [24]

Even though married to a planter who found practicality a desirable feminine trait, women were cautioned to exercise this talent only at home. They were not invited to join the Benevolent Society of Eufaula for fear that its duties "would be too much for their delicate frames." Instead they must practice Christian virtue in obedience to the sentiments of a typical toast of the 1830s: "Our Virtuous Fair—always lovely, but most so in the domestic circle." [25] Gentlemen were not to shock the sensibilities of these supposedly fragile creatures by uttering certain words (like "corset") in their presence. The opposite sex was adjured to be equally circumspect. Viola Goode Liddell recalled a spinster aunt who frequently visited the family home in Gastonburg and amused her nieces by requesting the "bosom" of the chicken, never the breast.[26]

Yet many such women had survived the rigorous journey down Federal Road and once resettled in Alabama defied Indians, snakes, and other perils of the wilderness. Their daughters exhibited similar fortitude when the Civil War threatened their hearths or husbands. Victoria Clayton accompanied her husband to "bleeding Kansas" and later visited him on many a battlefield, bringing homemade medicines and brandy for his comfort. The prospect of war inspired Mary Augusta Evans

Firor Scott, *The Southern Lady: From Pedestal to Politics, 1830–1930* (Chicago: University of Chicago Press, 1970).

24. Clayton, *White and Black,* pp. 42–43.

25. John Simpson Graham, *History of Clarke County* (Birmingham: Birmingham Printing Company, 1923), p. 136.

26. Liddell, *With a Southern Accent,* p. 13.

Wilson of Mobile to risk her father's disapproval by engaging in such an intellectual pursuit as writing. But her stern parent relented when *Beulah,* a rousing piece of southern propaganda, sold more than 20,000 copies in 1859.

When war touched Alabama, Mary Gordon Duffee, after tending soldiers wounded in the Federal raid on Brierfield, walked thirty miles back to her home in Elyton. Learning that her husband, Sen. Clement C. Clay, was imprisoned following the war, Virginia Clay journeyed to Washington to confront President Andrew Johnson and Secretary of War Edwin M. Stanton, demanding and eventually securing the senator's release. Many another Southern Lady of supposed "delicate frame" abandoned all pretense of helplessness and revealed her true mettle as an efficient manager quite equal to the task of running the plantation while her menfolk fought for the Confederacy.

But during the Victorian era and the early decades of the twentieth century, most Southern Ladies retreated to the safe harbors of home, church, and literary club, leaving only a relatively few daring souls to advocate woman's suffrage, prison reform, or the abolition of lynching and poll taxes. Carl Carmer described Alabama girls of the 1920s as virtually untouched by the morals revolution of that postwar era. He pictured them, much as Amelia Fry had depicted the women of early Cahaba, as simple-minded flirts who passed time in gossip, attired themselves in ruffled dresses, and engaged in a daily marathon of dating which began with lunch, afternoon, and supper dates, and continued into the night with early, regular, and late dates.

Carmer found southern males still toasting fair ladies, albeit more in jest than in solemnity. At one university function a slightly inebriated toastmaster, raising a glass of ice water, pronounced: "To woman, lovely woman of the Southland, as pure and chaste as this sparkling water, as cold as this gleaming ice, we lift this cup and we pledge our hearts and our lives to the protection of her virtue and chastity." Although fully aware that the spokesman was one of the most proficient seducers on campus, the audience heartily cheered his sentiment.[27]

27. Carmer, *Stars Fell on Alabama,* pp. 15–16.

Yet Carmer discovered another specimen of Alabama womankind whom he called Mary Louise. Married to a Black Belt lawyer, Mary Louise lived in a columned mansion, danced "expertly," and wore a few ruffles on the sleeves of her dress. She informed Carmer somewhat wistfully that she was "a type," one of many younger women of genteel birth who had dreamed of careers in music, art, or writing but eventually yielded, like their maternal ancestors, to the general expectation that marriage was their destiny.

Why has the Southern Lady been at the same time sublimated and glorified? John Temple Graves II offered the acute insight of a native southerner upon this contradiction. The fact that southern males are sensitive to women *as women,* he theorized, enhanced their masculinity. Yet southern *machismo* exacts its price. Graves described this cost poignantly: "The Southern male is a totalitarian about the female of the species . . . nearly always he is her master or her slave, rarely her comrade." [28]

Exemplars of the Southern Lady still consider it somewhat demeaning to accept money in return for work unless widowed and in dire straits. But those who continue to regard her as fragile have never witnessed her tremendous energy harnessed in behalf of a cause which she deems worthy. Those who still consider her of "delicate frame" have never faced the ferocity of her forehand nor marvelled at the accuracy with which she can place a chip shot on the green. She finds outlets for her talents and her natural aggression in volunteering for charity or in sports, no longer blushing to defeat a male opponent on the tennis court. So weep no more for the Southern Lady. She has long been liberated from the burdens of slaveholding and household drudgery. She possesses her college degree and her right to vote. She is still conditioned against pursuing a career other than that of wife and mother. But her daughter—or her granddaughter—may not prove so malleable.

Long before it became Alabama's capital, Montgomery was the Black Belt's unofficial capital, hub of its political, eco-

---

28. John Temple Graves II, *The Fighting South* (New York: G.P. Putnam's Sons, 1943), p. 213.

nomic, and social life. It shared this status to some extent with its satellite Selma, another river town only fifty miles distant. Montgomery served briefly as the Confederacy's capital, but Selma, a major arsenal in the lower South, eventually became even more important to this cause. Both were targets of the most extensive and damaging Union raid upon Alabama.

Exactly one hundred years after Wilson's Raiders swept through the Black Belt, another group of marchers trod the route between Selma and Montgomery. Whereas the 1865 raid had been a minor skirmish in the war to free the slaves, the 1965 march was an event of momentous consequence in the struggle for human rights. Was it mere happenstance that Montgomery and Selma found themselves in the path of such events? Or did their leadership, unyielding in defense of its lifestyle, shepherd them toward inevitable conflict and confrontation?

When Montgomery was incorporated in 1819 the primeval forest still protruded between the sixty-two houses and stores (most made of logs) which had sprung up at the confluence of Federal Road and the Alabama River.[29] Two groups of speculators had vied for this choice locale, wealthy politicians from "Georgy" versus vigorous New Englanders and easterners. When they finally united, Montgomery, the center of a slaveholding, landowning, cotton-growing economy, became Alabama's most important inland shipping point for cotton. During harvest, Court House Square was jammed with wagons, mules, horses, farmers, and brokers. Out of season, piles of decayed cottonseed testified to the overriding reason for Montgomery's existence.

From the beginning Montgomery was strongly influenced by a wealthy and genteel element which so regulated the community that it never experienced the raucous, shoot-'em-up phase of many a western village. Other pioneers, prospering in

29. The following material on Montgomery is drawn from Williams, "Early Ante-Bellum Montgomery: a Black-Belt Constituency"; Clanton W. Williams, "Conservatism in old Montgomery, 1817–1861," *Alabama Review* 10 (April 1957), 96–110; Arthur F. Howington, "Violence in Alabama: A Study of Late Ante-Bellum Montgomery," *Alabama Review* 27 (July 1974), 213–231.

Montgomery, smoothed away their rough edges to emulate the manner and customs of this dominant gentry. Although young Montgomery had a frontier facade, it was a decorous city where gaming devices were forbidden, slaves carefully patrolled, and a 9:00 P.M. curfew faithfully observed. While keeping tight rein over lawless elements, its leaders preferred to humiliate offenders by tarring and feathering them or dunking them in the river than by more extreme measures. No person was executed during Montgomery's first decade; only four murders were recorded between 1830 and 1840.

But as its population grew, Montgomery too partook of Alabama's addiction to violence. Although state law forbade the carrying of concealed weapons, Alabama ranked fifth among the thirty-one states in 1850 in the number of accidental deaths per capita caused by gunshot. This casual use of firearms and bowie knives was attributed to a frontier environment combined with a marked tendency on the part of Montgomerians, Alabamians, and southerners as a whole to settle disputes quickly, individually, and outside the law. An unwritten code sanctioned the white man's right to defend himself from insult or assault without fear of punishment.

Violence also stemmed from the subjugation of a black majority by a white minority increasingly fearful of general uprising or individual acts of vengeance. Its slave population exceeded that of whites in Montgomery County as early as 1830; by 1860 blacks outnumbered whites two to one. Montgomery grew ever more nervous, particularly at Christmas season when most field hands were idle. The Montgomery True Blues, Rifles, Cadets, and Dragoons, although also social organizations, existed primarily to form a citizen soldiery capable of putting down threats to the peculiar institution. Self-appointed vigilance committees kept watch for meddlesome abolitionists.

Within the city of Montgomery, whites slightly outnumbered their slaves. Early planters who often doubled as lawyers, physicians, journalists, bank or railroad directors, hotel or steamboat owners, and merchants had built their homes in town rather than on the lonely prairie. Numbers of Greek Revival mansions replaced the first log houses. Sociability flourished in this neighborly setting. Weekdays and evenings were enlivened by Masonic meetings, horseraces, raffles, circuses, theatricals, and balls.

Thriving Montgomery became a city with substantial interests in business, commerce, and manufacturing as well as cotton trading. As early as 1830 it was conservatively estimated that each of ninety planter families in town owned at least $5,000 in property. Per capita wealth of all free persons in Montgomery was more than $700, a figure never attained by the United States as a whole during the antebellum period. By 1846 Montgomery had become important enough to wrest the state capital away from Tuscaloosa.

Sons of pioneer planters had adopted the profession of law so enthusiastically that Montgomery, like other Black Belt counties, swarmed with attorneys. The ranks of physicians were almost as crowded. Such men were not only heirs to the plantation system but to the conviction that political control was their natural right and that they were eminently qualified to judge legislators, congressmen, governors, presidents, and court decisions. Although they might criticize their own institutions, they brooked no censure from outsiders, believing that only *they* understood the problems of their society. Proud, successful, and accustomed to leadership, this compact group, closely interwoven by marriage and kinship, marshalled its talents to secure its position.

Although this coterie united against outsiders, it divided internally for three decades. Politics, a subject of interest in Montgomery second only to cotton prices, ran the gamut from Jacksonian Democracy to Union Whiggery, from broad construction to nullification. But the rising challenge of abolitionism forced Montgomerians to choose between Henry W. Hilliard, who pleaded for harmony within the Union, and William Lowndes Yancey, who electrified listeners with his cry that "patriotism begins at home."

By 1860 the firebrand secessionist Yancey had prevailed. Montgomery, like every other county in the Black Belt and all but one in central and southern Alabama, voted to secede by such thumping majorities that reluctant elements in the hill country and wiregrass were overwhelmed. Convinced that the status quo could be maintained only by separation, 94 per cent of the voters of Montgomery cast ballots for secession, destining that their city should become the "cradle" of the Confederacy.

Like Montgomery, Selma had been founded by land speculators and had prospered as a river port, a center of the cotton economy, and a major slave mart. One of its founders, Sen. William Rufus King, who was to serve six weeks as vice-president of the United States in 1853, had given the town its Greek name, meaning seat or throne. As King had hoped, Selma did become the leading city of the western Black Belt. But despite King's strong Unionism and Democratic loyalties, Dallas County like Montgomery became a center of Whiggism after 1836.

In slaveholding, per capita wealth of its white population, and cotton production, Dallas outstripped Montgomery County. By 1850 it ranked first among Alabama's fifty-two counties in slaveholding. By 1856 its white citizens enjoyed a higher per capita wealth than whites of any other Alabama county. In 1860 Dallas led all Alabama counties in cotton production.

Even more rural than Montgomery County, Dallas was 76 percent black by 1860, a lopsided ratio which gave rise to frequent rumors of insurrection. Selma was rigidly patrolled, twenty-seven sections of its city code being devoted in 1860 to regulation of the black population. White males who served in volunteer militia and were heirs to a fighting tradition aimed at Indians and Mexicans welcomed the prospect of testing their marksmanship against that of Yankees.

Shortly after the election of Abraham Lincoln, Selma's male leadership gathered to debate its future course. Moderates urged consultation with other Southern states before taking the momentous step of leaving the Union but N. H. R. Dawson, a fiery young lawyer and leader of Selma's Minute Men, carried the day when fellow citizens, whooping and hollering, adopted his blunt resolution: "We, the citizens of Selma, are opposed to living under a government with a black Republican president." [30]

Selma's river and railroad connection and its location deep within the lower Confederacy made it a logical choice as a supply depot producing cannon, cartridges, shovels, horseshoe nails, uniforms, canteens, and other war needs in machine shops, iron mills, and cotton mills. Selma was the largest arsenal in the South save that of Richmond. By the spring of 1865, as the Confederacy's strength rapidly ebbed, Union Gen. James H. Wilson set out to destroy this remote base.

Opposed mostly by old men and boys, Wilson's troops swept into Selma, setting fire to its public buildings, storehouses, business district, and more than a hundred private homes; systematically destroying its industrial plants; and leaving Selma more heavily damaged than all other Alabama towns combined. In their exhilaration over the fall of Richmond, Northerners took little notice of Wilson's exploit but Selma's white citizens never forgot nor forgave those who laid waste their city.

Although slavery had ended, the descendants of chattels remained the majority in the Black Belt. A century after the start of the Civil War, blacks made up 80 percent of the population in Lowndes County and 78 percent of the population of Wilcox. But the white minority could not bring itself to accept the inevitable. In 1960 not a single black voted in either of these counties; only 0.9 percent of blacks in Dallas County and only 2,995 of 33,056 voting-age blacks in Montgomery County were registered.

The first voter discrimination case of the Kennedy administration, brought against Dallas County in 1961, ended substantially in failure. Other suits brought by the Justice Department met with frustrating delays and obstruction. Even the few black applicants who managed to reach Selma's board of registrars were rejected when they could not spell words like "emolument," "despotism," and "apportionment." After four years of litigation only 383 Dallas County blacks had been registered.

Casting about for a foil to dramatize the plight of disfranchised blacks, Martin Luther King, Jr., chose to focus upon

---

30. *Selma Times-Journal*, Centennial Edition, November 2, 1927.

Selma and Dallas County's irascible Sheriff James G. ("Jim") Clark. King's lieutenant, James Bevel, proposed the long march to the steps of Alabama's capitol to illustrate even more vividly the plight of the voteless. In the early spring of 1965, twelve days before the centennial of the fall of Selma, another liberating army marched toward Montgomery.

Cotton is still raised in the Black Belt but with expensive machinery stored in shiny metal barns rather than by men and women with hoes and hand plows. Soybeans are a major crop and cattle graze in many fields. In the pine barrens which form the southern border of this fertile land, timbering is a major occupation. Logs are piled precariously atop rickety trucks which make their way toward papermills in Wilcox County, Selma, Mobile, or Tuscaloosa, clogging traffic and intimidating ordinary motorists. The pine country is virtually untenanted except for occasional shacks or trailers inhabited by whites whose existence appears so humdrum and hopeless that it is easy to imagine them having piled into the dusty truck in 1965 and headed for Selma to jeer at the sight of blacks daring to demand their voting rights or to heckle "white niggers" from the North.

Since that time Selma and Montgomery have made a remarkable adjustment to the new realities of race relations, even going so far as to concede that Brown Chapel African Methodist Episcopal Church and Dexter Avenue Methodist Church are historic points which may prove equally as attractive to tourists as Sturdivant Hall or the first White House of the Confederacy. Both cities are meccas of trade, commerce, and recreation for residents of surrounding farmlands and small towns.

Montgomery is particularly compelling by virtue of its conviviality and the political stir generated each year when the legislature convenes. Scout troops, bands of clubwomen, and family groups tread the marble halls and visit the chambers of Alabama's intimate, old capitol where secessionists, Confederate legislators, and carpetbaggers once held forth. To examine their history further, these natives need only step next door to discover their archives, a veritable attic of the gentry crammed with such artifacts as Confederate swords, rifles, and uniforms;

stuffed owls and foxes; the fine chinaware and silver service once used by Vice-President King; old Mardi Gras costumes complete with crowns; inaugural ball gowns worn by governors' wives; even Charles Tait's wooden leg.

But in little towns of the pine barrens and the Black Belt, life is slowly ebbing away. Empty storefronts on main streets betray decay like toothless gaps in old men's mouths; the young, both black and white, seek more exciting worlds. Still, surprisingly, there are people living in hamlets like Pine Hill, Sunny South, Carlowville, Hurtsboro, and in county seats like Camden, selling hardware, dry goods, used cars, groceries, and gas, teaching, preaching, or practicing a little law, ginning cotton, operating sawmills, or doling out social security checks. (In one county with a population of 16,000, the Alabama Department of Pensions and Security had 14,000 cases on file during one recent year.) Even these activities come to a halt on Wednesdays or Thursdays when storekeepers traditionally pull down their shades, lock their doors, and take a midweek holiday to hunt, fish, engage in the newer pastime of golf on a course carved from cottonfield or pine forest, or simply nap in the shade of their side porches.

By late afternoon, heat has formed a haze behind which the sun disappears with a final, ferocious glare. Bullfrogs along the Alabama River and tree frogs in the pines set up their evening clatter. Night in the Black Belt, when the last drugstore within twenty-eight miles has extinguished its lights, exudes a special kind of loneliness. People, black and white, no longer distracted by their daily chores, must now confront their isolation, the almost total lack of diversion in their dark villages, the uneasy awareness that doctors are few and hospitals many miles distant, and, hauntingly, the ancient, brooding fears of each race for the other. ("Are the slaves rising?" "Is a rapist prowling the streets?" "Will the Klan ride tonight?" "Is a lynch mob gathering outside the jail?")

So they withdraw at dusk into the shelter of shack, trailer, sturdy brick ranch house, or ghostly mansion, dogs and guns close by, tall vapor lights creating little oases in the blackness. The dwindling gentry, like British colonials in the tropics, cling to little rituals of gracious living. For others there is nothing left but to enter the fantasy world of television or suffer the mindless chatter and plaintive music offered by radio disc jockeys in the neon-lit worlds of Selma, Montgomery, or Birmingham; or, these panaceas failing, to reach for time-honored solaces of the night, beer, bourbon, Bible, or warm body.

As cotton and slaves had inspired antebellum speculators, so coal, iron ore, and railroads lured the postwar venturesome. As men had once gambled for the most fertile soil of the Black Belt, they now prospected for the most promising seams beneath the red clay of the mineral region. Like the earlier wave of land seekers, these new entrepreneurs were optimistic, adventurous, and enterprising. Blaming agrarianism in part for the Confederacy's defeat, they not only dreamed of personal wealth but of a belated industrial revolution which would transform their devastated plantation economy into a prosperous New South.[31]

Sons and grandsons of pioneer Alabamians were among the first after the Civil War to explore the potential of mineral wealth: farmers' sons such as John T. Milner, James Withers Sloss, and Benjamin F. Roden; planters' sons such as Robert H. Henley and Henry F. DeBardeleben (whose name had been brought to this country by a Hessian ancestor hired by England to help put out the fires of revolution); and a grandson of the builder of Tannehill furnace named Thomas Tennessee Hillman.

Other prospectors were first-generation Alabamians who had migrated during the antebellum era in search of whatever opportunity might present itself. James R. Powell of Virginia had parlayed his horse, gun, and $20 into large landholdings and

31. Sources for the following brief summary of early Birmingham are Armes, *Story of Coal and Iron in Alabama;* Robert David Ward and William Warren Rogers, *Labor Revolt in Alabama, The Great Strike of 1894* (University, Ala.: University of Alabama Press, 1965); Allen Johnston Going, *Bourbon Democracy in Alabama, 1874–1890* (University, Ala.: University of Alabama Press, 1951); C. Vann Woodward, *Origins of the New South, 1877–1913* (Baton Rouge: Louisiana State University Press, 1951); and Carl Vernon Harris, "Economic Power and Politics: A Study of Birmingham, Alabama, 1890–1920" (Ph.D. diss., University of Wisconsin, 1970).

ownership of a mail coach line. Charles Linn, a Swede, had given up the adventurous life of a sea captain for the more sedate and prosperous profession of a merchant in Montgomery. Frank P. O'Brien, a native of Ireland, had run away from his Pennsylvania home at fourteen, drifted to Montgomery as a scenery painter, and arrived in Birmingham as a contractor. Josiah Morris of Maryland had already made large sums of money as a cotton broker in New Orleans before opening a private bank in Montgomery.

Milner, the "conscientious, plodding, savagely ambitious" [32] chief engineer of the South and North Railroad, was the first to anticipate that fortunes might be made by those who cornered the land where railroads would eventually cross in the midst of untapped deposits of coal and iron ore. From the crest of Red Mountain, the engineer pinpointed the future intersection of his road with the east-west lines of the Alabama and Chattanooga. His granddaughter later claimed that Milner had "a curious and remarkable dream sense" which had enabled him to envision the location of a "great workshop town." [33] Birmingham was not the creation of mystics, however, but of profit-minded men willing to risk boldly and unhesitatingly.

Powell, "argumentative," "dictatorial," [34] and in search of a new venture now that railroads had rendered stagecoaches obsolete, embellished Milner's idea. If railroads could be lured to cross at this spot, a "Magic City . . . a perfect Mahomet's paradise of lovely women," [35] would spring up. "The Duke of Birmingham," with his snowy hair, hawk nose, and air of command, shared Milner's faith in the "staring, bold, mean little town" [36] which its promoters optimistically named Birmingham. But a less imaginative man needed to fortify himself with a full quart of whiskey before he could foresee that this straggling array of yellow pine shacks and boxcars would become a major metropolis of the New South.

32. Armes, *Coal and Iron in Alabama*, p. 110.
33. Armes, *Story of Coal and Iron*, p. 219.
34. Armes, *Story of Coal and Iron*, p. 223.
35. Armes, *Story of Coal and Iron*, p. 234.
36. Armes, *Story of Coal and Iron*, p. 234.

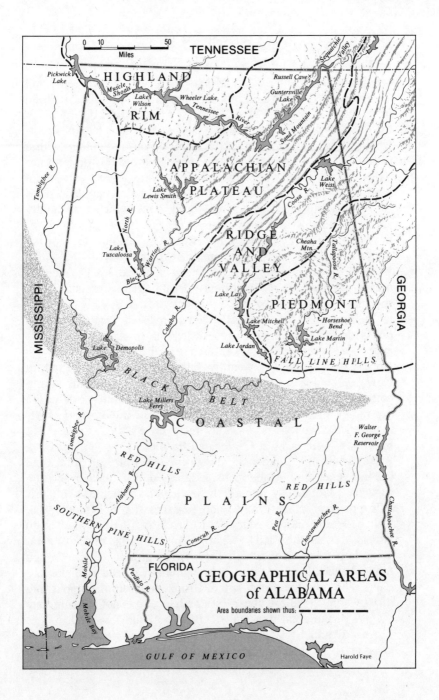

GEOGRAPHICAL AREAS
of ALABAMA

Area boundaries shown thus: ▬ ▬ ▬

Harold Faye

On the strength of Milner's plan, Powell's talent for grandi-
ose promotion, and Josiah Morris's money, the Elyton Land
Company in 1871 offered lots surrounding the proposed railroad
intersection at $75 to $150. Major A. Marre paid $100 for a 50-
by-100-foot lot at First Avenue, North, and Nineteenth Street,
which would be worth no less than fifty thousand dollars within
twenty years. Charles Linn paid a premium $400 for a corner
close by the point where the railroads were to cross the main
north-south business street. Virtually the entire populace jibed
at "Linn's Folly," a three-story brick bank which rose boldly
above the shacks. But forty years later, this corner of First Avenue, North, and Twentieth Street would be headquarters for the
major coal, steel, and iron interests of the Southeast.

As the best cotton land had been snapped up by men of
means, pioneer enterprises of early Birmingham were started by
speculators who, like Powell, Linn, and Morris, already had capital behind them. Benjamin Roden reinvested the proceeds of
his Gadsden grocery and timber interests in real estate, insurance, and street railway ventures in Birmingham. Henry F.
DeBardeleben and his wealthy father-in-law, Daniel Pratt, a
New England carpenter who had prospered by manufacturing
cotton gins and textiles in Autauga County, acquired title to the
ore mines and antebellum furnaces around Oxmoor. T. T. Hillman on his twenty-first birthday received a $50,000 interest in
his family's furnaces at Center and Empire.

Birmingham's founders, an intimate circle of first- and
second-generation Alabamians, addressed one another by title
(usually "Colonel"), regarded the mayor's office as their private preserve, named mines and furnaces for their womenfolk
(Alice, Hattie, Lady, Mary Pratt), and left their surnames on
streets, hotels, hospitals, schools, and suburbs of the "great
workshop town" for which they broke ground. But although
many bequeathed valuable Birmingham real estate to descendants who now live in Mountain Brook, far from the smoke and
dirt of Jones Valley, these city fathers were not the ultimate
owners of the great iron and steel industry they sparked.

As "Colonel" Milner had schemed, railroads eventually
crossed Birmingham. Fortune seekers bought lots and erected

five hundred homes and stores along the broad, muddy streets. But their dreams of quick profit from real estate and mineral freight were punctured in 1873 by the devastating effects of a nationwide depression and a local cholera epidemic. "Colonel" Powell packed up and moved to Mississippi, where he founded another town called Belzoni, experimented with scientific farming, and was shot to death by an angry man whom he had discharged as a plantation manager. The city he had envisioned did not show signs of magical growth until eight years after boosters had staked out its streets and lots. With the lifting of depression, northern and English capital sought new investments in a South restored to native conservative leaders hospitable to business enterprise.

Birmingham's boom began with the discovery that good quality pig iron could be made by combining coking coal with local iron ore. The first reliable supply of coking coal was developed in 1879 by Pratt Coal and Coke Company owned by "Colonel" DeBardeleben, "Colonel" Sloss, and a mining engineer from New York, Truman H. Aldrich. This vigorous newcomer had entered the Alabama coal fields in 1873 with a dramatic flare, ordering his Montevallo miners to the unprecedented act of digging coal in midsummer. ("No one ever knew what a Yankee would do next!" commented Ethel Armes.[37]) With Montevallo coal piled high on the ground when the first sharp bite of winter came, orders poured in as never before.

Eager to reinvigorate its struggling venture, the Elyton Land Company virtually donated prime sites near the railroad juncture to induce DeBardeleben and Sloss to build new pig iron furnaces and Kentucky ironmasters to construct a rolling mill. The Louisville and Nashville Railroad, under energetic Milton Hannibal Smith, took over the ailing South and North line, pumped capital into industrial ventures, and gave freight-rate concessions to all.

New furnaces, enjoying easy access to coal, iron ore, and railroads, plus an ample supply of cheap black labor, soon produced pig iron at the lowest cost in America and undersold Eng-

37. Armes, *Story of Coal and Iron*, p. 271.

lish pig iron in England. Alabama coal production climbed
even more rapidly.

Another trend, that of absentee ownership, began after the
breakup in 1881 of the partnership of DeBardeleben, Sloss, and
Aldrich, captains of the Old Guard. Aldrich concentrated on
coal mining, Sloss on furnaces, but DeBardeleben, in the erro-
neous belief that he was suffering from tuberculosis, sold the
Pratt Company to "Colonel" Enoch Ensley and a group of Tennessee capitalists in the first million-dollar deal of the Birmingham district.

After only five years, Enoch Ensley and his associates were
bought out in turn by the Tennessee Coal, Iron and Railroad
Company. This Tennessee-based concern proceeded to absorb
Aldrich's vast Cahaba coal mining interests as well as DeBardeleben's later creation, the DeBardeleben Coal and Iron Company, capitalized in 1889 at $10,000,000. "I had been the eagle
eating the crawfish," DeBardeleben remarked philosophically.
"Now a bigger eagle . . . came along and swallowed me." [38]
DeBardeleben and Aldrich became officers of TCI's newly
consolidated holdings but in 1894 Aldrich resigned to run for
Congress and DeBardeleben was forced out of TCI's vice-
presidency after he had sought unsuccessfully to gain majority
control of the corporation's stock.

By 1900 most of Birmingham's small iron companies had
also been forced by price competition to merge into three ab-
sentee-owned corporations: Sloss-Sheffield Steel and Iron Company, Republic Iron and Steel Company, and Woodward Iron
Company. But TCI was by far Alabama's largest and most powerful coal and iron company, owning thirteen furnaces, all fed
from its own mines, and a princely domain of 400,000 acres of
coal and iron lands. Of its 210,000 shares of stock in 1900, only
660 were held by Alabamians; only one man from Birmingham
served on its seventeen-member board of directors.

Other industrial enterprises in northern Alabama underwent a
similar shift of ownership. Encouraged by Birmingham's success, promoters started booms in twenty or more towns between

---

38. Armes, *Story of Coal and Iron*, p. 424.

1885 and the early 1890s. Some of the larger ventures were located in Anniston, Gadsden, and Sheffield. Assisted by capital from New York and from Daniel Tyler, a former Union general, Samuel Noble began making car wheel iron in a little town originally called Woodstock. Its name changed to honor the wife of one of its financial backers, Anniston was welcomed to the New South in 1883 by none other than Henry W. Grady himself.

Operations at Sheffield, begun by a native Alabamian Walter Moore and by "Colonel" Ensley, were later taken over by the Tennessee Coal, Iron and Railroad Company and by Sloss-Sheffield. Gadsden, whose early promoter "Colonel" Robert B. Kyle started a furnace company in the 1880s, later became a manufacturing headquarters for the Republic Iron and Steel Company.

Although Birmingham was recognized as the industrial capital of the New South, its coming of age had been marred by fierce strife between labor and management. This was more than the normal tension between workers and employers. Birmingham's labor force was a volatile mix of social hostilities and economic rivalries: native poor whites, former slaves, and recent immigrants from the British Isles, Italy, and southern Europe all jostling for jobs. To complicate matters further, union labor competed against nonunion labor and free miners against convict laborers.

The use of state and county convicts as a cheap, captive labor force for industry had grown out of a truce between planter interests of the Black Belt and new industrialists. Agrarian leaders, rightly suspecting that Birmingham's jobs would lure their tenants and sharecroppers away from the cotton fields, initially fought the boom town and damned the New South as a phrase of "Yankee invention." The mineral region, underrepresented in the legislature after its population grew, complained that baldheaded "old fogies" in the Black Belt, ruling over powerless black majorities, had more than their share of legislative seats and influence. But men of property, whether industrial or agricultural, eventually made common cause. Convict leasing, being profitable to industry and saving taxes for all, was one result. Julia Tutwiler, an aristocratic maiden lady turned social reformer, bluntly described convict leasing in the 1890s as combining "all the evils of slavery without one of its ameliorating features." [39]

TCI received an exclusive ten-year contract in 1888 to employ all state convicts, compensating the state from $9 to $18 a month per man. The company also shared Jefferson County convicts with Sloss-Sheffield Steel and Iron Company. In vain Alabama's free miners protested that convict labor took jobs away from them, kept wages low, and served as a reserve work force to break strikes. The Knights of Labor, attempting strikes in the Birmingham area during the 1880s, met with almost total failure primarily because strikers could so easily be replaced by convicts, nonunion labor, or by imported strikebreakers called "blacklegs."

Nationwide labor unrest aroused by the depression of 1894 was reflected in a major test of strength between owners and some seven thousand striking miners in Alabama's mineral district. Strikers dynamited Horse Creek Mines in Walker County and later killed three blacklegs and a guard in what was dubbed "the Pratt Massacre." Gov. Thomas Goode Jones, responding to appeals from industrialists who had supported his election, ordered the state militia to encamp in Ensley for almost three months as a warning against further armed demonstrations.

Throughout this uneasy summer, DeBardeleben, then TCI vice-president, served as chief strategist for the operators, using strikebreakers freely, importing black labor from as far away as Kansas, blacklisting men who struck, and attempting to replace the aroused white miners with more subservient black workers. Purportedly to lessen the oversupply of labor, he even offered strikers free transportation to the Ohio mine fields. Populist and union leaders suspected that this was not so much a gesture of largesse as an effort to remove miners who might vote for Reuben F. Kolb, Populist candidate for governor.

As historians later viewed the 1894 strike, all parties had enacted classic roles in a script of industrial warfare as written during the 1890s. Industry stoutly resisted any participation by

39. McMillan, *Land Called Alabama*, p. 296.

labor in determining wages or rents. DeBardeleben, representing this general view, proved an inventive antagonist, not so much hostile to labor as determined that the companies should survive. Governor Jones, emulating President Grover Cleveland's hard line against Eugene V. Debs's American Railway Union, took firm action to suppress labor agitation. Many Birmingham citizens, alarmed at the violence within their community, approved Jones's stand.

Faced with such odds, the strikers finally capitulated. Unions would attempt to make gains in Birmingham during the first decade of the twentieth century and after the First World War but would register no sustained progress until the mid-1930s. The leasing of convicts to private industry would not end in Alabama until the first administration of Bibb Graves, elected in 1926 as the neo-Populist candidate of another plain peoples' movement.

Those convicts who survived their sentences in the mines usually remained in the area, adding to the unsavory reputation of "Bad Birmingham." Since the 1880s Birmingham had been widely regarded as the most crime-ridden city for its size in the nation, the number of arrests each year between 1888 and 1908 being roughly equivalent to one-third of its total population. This statistic was misleading. Birmingham's police jurisdiction extended beyond the city limits to mining districts like Beer Mash, Buzzard's Roost, Scratch Ankle, and Hole-in-the-Wall; the rowdyism of such areas was reflected in the city's crime rate. Also Jefferson County paid its law officials a fee for each person arrested or sentenced, thereby rewarding zealotry in rounding up offenders guilty of shooting dice, betting on cards, and other minor transgressions.

Alarmed citizens, however, began to remove themselves from proximity to the crime and grime engendered by the industries they owned. Once-fashionable Fifth Avenue, North, was abandoned in favor of South Highlands, a new residential area on higher ground at the foot of Red Mountain. Victorian gingerbread mansions and pseudo-Athenian temples later stretched along the curves of Highland Avenue to make that street, so Birmingham claimed, the most imposing residential avenue in the South. Upper-income residents would eventually erect copies of Tudor or Mediterranean mansions on the crest of Red Mountain overlooking the city which John T. Milner had foreseen. Before this summit was reached, the reins of Birmingham power had passed into new hands.

Faced with a slump in the pig iron market, the Tennessee Company had built its first open-hearth steel plant in Ensley in 1899. Within a few years this plant was turning out most of the railroad rails of the United States. In 1907 TCI received an order which "riveted the attention of the entire steel world on the new Ensley plant": E. H. Harriman wanted 150,000 tons of open-hearth rails to supply his entire railroad network.[40] Looking south, the Pittsburgh steel masters and their New York bankers foresaw the rise of a major competitor.

When panic threatened the American financial world in 1907, J. Pierpont Morgan, Elbert H. Gary, and Henry C. Frick moved to take this upstart under the wing of the giant United States Steel Corporation by purchasing all but a fraction of TCI's stock from an ailing New York bank firm. The purchase was represented to an acquiescent President Theodore Roosevelt and to the American people as a public service to prevent the spread of panic. In actuality U.S. Steel had seized an opportunity to acquire the tremendous ore and coal deposits of TCI (which one authority on trusts conservatively estimated to be worth a billion dollars) for $35,317,632.

Senate investigators scolded Roosevelt for presuming that he had the authority to permit an absorption which violated the Sherman Anti-Trust Act. U.S. Steel, the Senate committee charged, had acquired monopolies of the open-hearth output of steel rails, the national supply of iron ore, and the iron and steel trade of the South while taking over a threatening competitor. As DeBardeleben, with his gift for a picturesque phrase might have put it, the biggest eagle of them all had swooped down on Birmingham.

Warren G. Harding paid a courtesy call on Birmingham to mark its semicentennial in 1921. But even this presidential ges-

---

40. Armes, *Story of Coal and Iron*, p. 515.

ture could not obscure the fact that Birmingham had not achieved its vaunted potential. It was still the "great workshop town" rather than the cosmopolitan metropolis of the South, a youthful braggart more akin to Tulsa and Oklahoma City than to self-assured mature neighbors like New Orleans, Atlanta, or Nashville.

The overwhelming majority of its people were working-class, sparsely educated, economically insecure, and racially divided. Still strongly influenced by their rural origins and a lingering tradition of frontier individualism, many of these white laborers hamstrung unionism by valuing the right to work more highly than union loyalty in times of strikes. Blacks, being pawns of the fee system and convict leasing, were economically as well as politically impotent.

Efforts by middle-level merchants, real estate agents, professionals, and independent businessmen to institute civic improvements which might prove costly to the dominant railroads and industries invariably failed. Birmingham's top leadership had also displayed a nimble ability to avoid efforts to raise property taxes, end convict leasing, or control the pollution from smokestacks. Yet most citizens of every strata agreed that Birmingham's industries must operate fullblast and unimpeded if their city were ever to overtake its rivals.[41]

But as the twenties approached a crashing finale, smoke ceased to pour from the stacks of Birmingham's mills and factories. In June 1929, four Jefferson County banks closed, signalling the onset of deep and prolonged depression. The Great Depression hit Birmingham early, paralyzed its heavy industry, and cast one-third of its people upon the mercy of unprepared and inadequate private welfare. During the 1930s Birmingham was frequently described as "the hardest hit city in the nation."[42] (The Communist party, hoping to sow seeds of revolution in this fertile ground, made its southern headquarters in Birmingham.) Congressman George Huddleston, pleading for

41. Harris, "Economic Power and Politics," pp. 465–480.
42. George R. Leighton, "Birmingham, Alabama: The City of Perpetual Promise," *Harper's* 175 (August 1937): 239.

federal relief to his stricken city, told a congressional committee that it was not fair to expect Birmingham, whose major industries were owned in the North, to cope with its monumental relief problems unaided.

Originally Birmingham's leadership had attempted to care for its own. In deciding what was best for their people, this elite followed traditions of paternalism and self-reliance deeply rooted in the southern ethic. While Old Master had dispensed his largesse single-handedly, his philosophical heirs, a coterie of the city's business leaders, shared this responsibility among themselves. They set the limits of charity and apportioned it as they saw fit, proving reluctant to admit blacks, organized labor, women, or professional social workers to their innermost councils. By co-ordinating within a Community Chest, they experienced the satisfactions of philanthropy while protecting themselves from a multiplicity of appeals.[43]

But even though the chest raised a record $750,000 within eight days in 1931, it proved unable to cope with the rising need for relief. By 1933 almost a hundred thousand persons jammed Birmingham's relief rolls. Chest leaders, their voluntary resources exhausted, welcomed a loan from the Reconstruction Finance Corporation to avert the possibility of actual starvation in their community. Despite Franklin Roosevelt's early warning that welfare would be centered at Washington or state capitals if private organizations cut back, Birmingham's leadership relinquished the burden of relief to the federal government with alacrity.

World War II revived Birmingham industry but, at war's end, the once-magic city relapsed again. Birmingham in 1947 had no local symphony orchestra, chamber music society, community theater, outstanding parks, or downtown men's club. Even its zoo had closed. Despite an abundance of empty war plants, no major industry had chosen to locate in the area since the Axis defeat. Schools and other public services were starved by a low property tax structure. But the root of this torpor, many civic

43. Edward S. LaMonte, "Politics and Welfare in Birmingham, 1900–1974" (Ph.D. diss., University of Chicago, 1976), pp. 145–165.

promoters insisted, was absentee ownership of major industries.[44]

Critics began to voice publicly a complaint which had been
whispered privately for decades: the United States Steel Corporation, although directly employing 40,000 Birmingham
workers and indirectly responsible for thousands of other jobs,
treated Birmingham like a southern stepchild in order to protect
its holdings in the East. Despite lower costs of labor and raw
materials, Birmingham's ingot steel was priced three dollars a
ton higher than that of Pittsburgh. This artificially high price,
coupled with southern freight rates which favored the shipping
of raw rather than finished materials, accounted for the fact that
the annual steel ingot capacity of TCI's antiquated furnaces had
expanded only 600,000 tons in twenty years.

Many suspected, furthermore, that United States Steel had ac-
tively blocked other industries which might compete for labor
and cause Birmingham's low-wage structure to rise. Local merchants were aggrieved because the steel corporation persisted in
paying its workers in "clacker," a metal scrip redeemable only
at company stores, until forced to discontinue this practice at the
start of World War II. Those concerned with city financing
complained that United States Steel placed its mills and offices
carefully outside the tax limits of Birmingham and fought any
move to absorb these municipalities or unincorporated areas into
the central city.

Birmingham's historic disadvantages in marketing steel were
removed in the late 1940s. The Interstate Commerce Commission equalized freight rates and the Supreme Court made clear
that it would no longer tolerate a pricing system which enriched
some plants at the expense of others. But although its economic
prospects brightened, Birmingham faced an even graver concern. The Supreme Court served notice in 1954 that drastic
changes in racial mores loomed ahead.

Birmingham in the 1950s was the nation's largest and most
rigid bastion of segregation. Theaters, restaurants, hotels, and

---

44. Irving Beiman, "Birmingham: Steel Giant with a Glass Jaw," in Robert S.
Allen, ed., *Our Fair City* (New York: Vanguard Press, Inc., 1947), pp. 99–122.

cemeteries were separated as to race; elevators, water fountains, and rest rooms were marked "white" or "colored," and the financially hard-pressed city struggled to maintain two sets of schools, libraries, parks, and hospital facilities. Although Memphis, Nashville, Atlanta, and Mobile each had a sprinkling of black policemen, none served on Birmingham's force. Not a single black doctor practiced in the "white" hospitals nor belonged to the Jefferson County Medical Society. Only in the areas of voting, wage scales, and social welfare—all fostered by Washington—had Birmingham's blacks made progress since the start of the twentieth century.

An attempt to launch a Birmingham chapter of the National Urban League had failed in 1949 when business and civic leaders withdrew their financial blessing. (A chapter of the Urban League had been organized in Atlanta as early as 1919 and was supported by that city's Community Chest.) The sole avenue for dialogue between the races, an interracial committee within one Community Chest agency, was disbanded by chest leaders in 1955 after white supremacists threatened to boycott the entire fund-raising campaign. Thus Birmingham entered the era of racial revolution without a single channel of communication through which whites and blacks might negotiate.[45]

Faced by an edict that schools must eventually be integrated and by challenges to the entire public structure of segregation, some of Birmingham's more moderate leaders adopted a posture of resisting change by legal strategems (such as "freedom-of-choice" laws for schools). But in general the city's leadership evidenced what has been described by students of this era as "*non*decision making" and "the politics of *non*-politics." Charles Morgan, Jr., an outspoken critic of the Birmingham establishment, later claimed that its members "passionately did *not* want to lead." Dr. Martin Luther King, Jr., after demonstrating that Birmingham could be used as a dramatic foil for civil rights demonstrations, concluded that the city's ultimate

45. LaMonte, "Politics and Welfare in Birmingham, 1900–1974," p. 231.

tragedy had not been the brutality of its "bad" people but the silence of its "good" people.[46]

No matter what labels were attached to it, this attitude persisted for almost a decade during which Birmingham's image was increasingly darkened by bombings and rioting. Ordered to integrate recreational facilities, the city government closed sixty-eight parks, thirty-eight playgrounds, six swimming pools, and four golf courses. The Birmingham Bar Association, debating whether to urge compliance with the law, finally voted to take no position in the matter. When blacks boycotted downtown stores to demand an end to segregated customs, the major merchants, caught between their black and white customers, proved unable to act.

Observing that the power structure refused to seek change openly, other men stepped into the void. The Young Men's Business Club, a maverick group of younger professionals and businessmen, took on the project, recommended by the Birmingham Bar Association, of changing Birmingham's form of government from commission to mayor-council. This movement was headed by two young attorneys, Erskine Smith and David Vann, both of whom had roots in Birmingham which went back for almost a century. Publicly this was described as a means of persuading suburbs to merge with Birmingham. But implicit in the proposed change was the hope of creating a better racial climate by replacing Eugene "Bull" Connor and his fellow commissioners with more tractable heads of city government. An alarmed Connor warned his followers that Vann, who had once served as law clerk to Supreme Court Justice Hugo Black, had been sent by Black "to brainwash us." [47] Nonetheless, by a thin margin of 777 out of 36,400 votes, Birmingham citizens agreed to try the mayor-council system.

This action was a major turning point for Birmingham even though its immediate result was chaos at city hall. Albert Bout-

---

46. Michael Nichols, "Cities Are What Men Make Them: Birmingham Faces the Civil Rights Movement, 1963" (senior honors thesis, Brown University, 1974), p. 180.
47. LaMonte, "Politics and Welfare in Birmingham," pp. 226, 242.

well, chosen for his moderation, defeated Connor for mayor in April 1963, but "Bull" and his fellow commissioners contested the mayor-council election. For six weeks that spring, while Birmingham was in the grip of its most intense racial crisis, no one was clearly in charge of city government. Awaiting a decision by the Alabama Supreme Court, both groups of officials claimed the right to govern.

Although the majority of Birmingham's whites had signalled a willingness to make some racial accommodation, Dr. King decided to proceed with a massive display of nonviolent resistance by Birmingham's young blacks. On May 3, 1963, Connor ordered the use of firehoses and police dogs against the demonstrators. This action, pictured in countless newspapers and on millions of television screens, evoked a national storm of outrage and brought on a summit meeting between local black leaders and seventy-seven of the most powerful white men in Birmingham, with the federal government acting as broker. Within a week a settlement was reached. In effect Birmingham white leadership abandoned total intransigence. Downtown was desegregated, better jobs promised to blacks, and all demonstrators were to be released from jail.

While negotiations were underway, both groups claiming to govern Birmingham had decried them. City commissioners described the white business leaders as "a bunch of quisling, gutless traitors." [48] The city council swore "no surrender" on the issue of segregation.[49] Downtown merchants denied any part in discussions of desegregating their own facilities. Only one member of the seventy-seven so-called Senior Citizens Committee, Sidney W. Smyer, whose ties with Birmingham stretched back to its founding by the Elyton Land Company, allowed his name to be publicly identified with the discussion. Eventually the names of the seventy-seven whites were released with no indication of who had attended meetings or what role any of them had played in the settlement. After the Alabama Supreme Court confirmed the election of Boutwell and the

48. LaMonte, "Politics and Welfare in Birmingham," p. 258.
49. LaMonte, "Politics and Welfare in Birmingham," p. 259.

council, the Senior Citizens Committee disbanded as quietly as
it had appeared.

Why had the leadership of Birmingham proven so timid at a
time when their city's archrival Atlanta was proclaiming itself
"too busy to hate" and when moderate reform was taking place
peaceably in Charleston, Mobile, Nashville, and Memphis?

Each of these other southern cities had a longer history during
which to develop a deeply rooted aristocracy imbued with a
sense of responsibility for the conduct of community affairs.
(Charleston was founded in the seventeenth century, Mobile and
Nashville in the eighteenth, and Memphis and Atlanta well before the Civil War.) In early Birmingham, social prestige came
almost entirely from economic success. James Bowron, who
came to Birmingham from Nashville in 1895 as treasurer of the
Tennessee Coal, Iron and Railroad Company, was somewhat astonished to find that the iron trade was respectable in his new
home city. "In Nashville . . . I have never taken any com-
manding position in the social life," he wrote. "In Birmingham, I found it was not so much a question of what a man's
grandfather had been, but the question was and still is, 'what
does he do?' " In short, the men with the most economic power
in Birmingham also enjoyed the highest social status.[50]

Descendants of Alabama pioneers had founded Birmingham,
but these first families had lost their grip on the reins of power
as local industries were absorbed into national corporations.
Being predominantly an industrial center, Birmingham found itself led in large part by managers rather than owners. The majority of this managerial group, schooled in industrial techniques
rather than humanistic studies, viewed Birmingham from an immediate rather than a long-range perspective. Primarily concerned with extracting from the city rather than with building it,
they feared that racial change would prove politically and financially detrimental to the interests which they represented.

It is more difficult to account for the silence of those in Birmingham whose forebears were Alabama's pioneer planters and

50. Harris, "Economic Power and Politics," pp. 69–70.

ironmasters. Yet this very description of their heritage contains certain clues. These were the sons and grandsons of soldiers of fortune, materialistic men who cleared the canebrake and plumbed the seams of coal and iron. From Philip Gosse in the 1850s to Carl Carmer in the 1920s, numerous observers had noted that this leadership, for all its professed love of culture, had no deep commitment to intellectualism. Theirs was a heritage of hot rhetoric rather than the cooler, measured process of committing thought to written form.

Henry Adams, that introspective New England Brahmin, scorned the young southerners of gentle birth whom he met at Harvard in the 1850s, describing them as attractive yet essentially uncomplex men, accustomed to command but not to the stern discipline of scholarly inquiry, more temperamental than thoughtful. Even some fellow southerners, when able to view their peers objectively, remarked on this trait. Clarence Cason commented that most Alabama men read newspapers avidly in search of political, financial, and social items but regarded books as suitable only for invalids. Wilbur J. Cash, after brooding on the southern psyche for more than a decade, concluded that the typical southerner "did not . . . think; he felt; and discharging his feelings immediately, he developed no need or desire for intellectual culture in its own right." [51]

(A hasty disclaimer should be made at this point; social conscience does not *invariably* arise from acquaintance with the history, philosophy, or literature of mankind. But there is an ominous element of truth in the often-quoted warning of the philosopher George Santayana that those who do not study the past are doomed to repeat it.)

Nonintellectualism is only one facet of many a southerner's philosophical heritage. Prof. Sheldon Hackney, native of Birmingham, president of Tulane University, and a leading scholar of southern violence, has identified a "siege mentality" within his fellows.[52] Their strong regional consciousness, he theorizes,

51. Cash, *Mind of the South*, p. 102.
52. Sheldon Hackney, "Southern Violence," *American Historical Review* 74 (February 1969): 906–925.

stems from resistance to all those whom they have considered meddlesome intruders: abolitionists, the Union army, carpetbaggers, feminists, Darwinists, trade unionists, Socialists, Communists, advocates of daylight saving time, representatives of Wall Street, Pittsburgh, and Washington, and, most recently, civil rights advocates.

In fighting off these incursions, many southerners developed a world view which, Hackney suggests, "defines the social, political, and physical environment as hostile." [53] Associating new ideas with malevolent forces from outside, many a southern leader has abdicated responsibility for change. In Hackney's words:

> From the southern past arise the symbiosis of profuse hospitality and intense hostility toward strangers, and the paradox that the southern heritage is at the same time one of grace and violence.[54]

Other than these intangible influences, there were certain concrete reasons for the dearth of leadership by men of financial power and social prestige. Although agricultural and economic leaders had dominated Alabama's governorship and senatorial seats until the mid-1920s, Birmingham's elite had not made it a practice to occupy the mayor's office. After the first cozy circle of founders dispersed, most of Birmingham's mayors from 1871 to 1953 were middle-ranking businessmen who had worked their way up from professions like mechanic, carpenter, rolling mill worker, schoolteacher, salesman, and scenery painter. Only J. A. Van Hoose (1895–1897) and George B. Ward (1905–1909, 1913–1917) had been members of the upper economic echelon.[55] Representatives of the power structure frequently occupied Jefferson County's sole seat in the state senate before reapportionment but had forsaken the mayor's chair, preferring to work behind the scenes to choose and influence its occupant.

Many men of power were also ineligible to run for mayor because they resided in the bedroom suburb of Mountain Brook,

53. Hackney, "Southern Violence," p. 924.
54. Hackney, "Southern Violence," p. 925.
55. Harris, "Economic Power and Politics," pp. 125–128.

a wooded fastness among the Appalachian foothills with a beauty almost unmatched among suburbs of American cities. Its inmost elite congregate at the Mountain Brook Country Club, a copy of the plantation mansion rendered larger than life and embellished with tennis courts and a golf course.

By contrast, Atlanta faced the civil rights turbulence of the early 1960s under the mayoralty of Ivan Allen, Jr., a millionaire business leader and member of its social elite, who helped desegregate its hotels, parks, and swimming pools and upon at least one occasion personally quelled an impending riot. (The psychiatrist Robert Coles, discussing why desegregation riots took place in New Orleans but not in Atlanta, suggested that this was due to the insistence of Atlanta's leadership upon cool response. Coles postulated that the masses tend to follow forthright moral leadership despite their previous prejudices.[56])

Birmingham's leaders were somewhat ashamed of "Bull" Connor, snubbed him socially, but allowed "Bull" and his followers (as previous generations of Alabama leaders had allowed Klansmen and lynch mobs) to guard the ramparts against agents of change. Thus when the civil rights crisis confronted Birmingham, "Bull" Connor rather than its elite represented their city before the world.

Birmingham finally resolved its agony at the insistence of men whose feelings for the city were anchored deep in its past. David Vann was politically ambitious but this was not his sole motivation. As "Bull" Connor had warned, Vann had a genuine commitment to furthering social justice. Sidney W. Smyer was more representative of the older leadership. Smyer found the courage to appear in a public role through a mixture of motives: his realistic appraisal of the eventual outcome of the crisis, his financial involvement with Birmingham's future, and his sense of outrage at the way in which the world perceived a city which his forebears had helped to found. He himself explained it, not in elegant or intellectual terms but in the blunt-spoken, pragmatic southern traditon: "I'm a segregationist but I'm not a damn fool!" [57]

*

56. Quoted in Nichols, "Birmingham Faces the Civil Rights Movement," p. 182.
57. *Birmingham News,* Centennial Section, December 19, 1971.

Save for the enduring presence of Red Mountain, John T. Milner, James R. Powell, and Josiah Morris might not recognize their "great workshop town" in 1976. The optimistic Powell would not be astonished by its physical growth. Milner would find a familiar landmark in the old Sloss furnace, still at its original site near the railroad tracks, although slated to be razed in the interest of progress. Morris would find his name emblazoned on one of the original downtown streets, recently restored and occupied by a string of restaurants and nightclubs catering to tourists and Birmingham's younger citizens. But if the founders could observe Birmingham's racial behavior, they might well think that their eyes deceived them.

Once the most tightly segregated city in the nation, downtown Birmingham by 1976 was thoroughly integrated. Almost as if it had always been this way, blacks share schools, parks, libraries, restaurants, and hotels, hold responsible positions in offices and stores, serve on Birmingham's police force and city council, debating freely, if they choose, with Mayor David Vann.

Younger generations of whites and blacks find it hard to believe their elders' tales of "white" and "colored" signs on water fountains, bus seats, elevators, and rest rooms. But for members of both races who reached adulthood before 1963, the transformation of Birmingham is akin to a miracle.

This is not to claim that widespread social integration has come about. Although blacks and whites may mix socially at will, members of the two races generally tend to keep to their separate neighborhoods, clubs, churches, and lifestyles. Well-to-do whites in Mountain Brook continue to live in almost total residential segregation save for the daylight presence of maids, gardeners, and caddies.

Both races, moreover, have accepted their daily elbow-rubbing with a grace which neither would have dreamed possible twenty years ago. The smoothness with which the white South acceded to integration when the die was finally cast has been the envy of many a northern community. How was such a turnabout possible at a time when holier-than-thou Yankees were finding racial accommodation so difficult?

Some trace this to the personal friendship which has always

crossed racial lines in the South, perhaps patronizing on the part of whites or subservient on the part of blacks, but nonetheless real. Others attribute it to the sunny side of southerners, the genuine warmth and kindness which has coexisted alongside fear, passion, and hatred in their psyche. Perhaps it has something to do with the neighborly quality of southern life, a luxury almost entirely lost to the lonely crowd on the eastern seaboard.

Whatever the reasons for Birmingham's acceptance of change, the city achieved a better quality of life in the crossing of its Rubicon. Racial peace has been followed by prosperity. Despite the recession of 1974–1975, Birmingham's business structure held up better than that of many another city of its size. Although heavy industry cut back, employment rose in the areas of wholesale and retail trade, finance, and government. While United States Steel is still the largest employer in Jefferson County, the largest employer within Birmingham itself is the rapidly expanding campus of the University of Alabama in Birmingham, with its schools of medicine, dentistry, nursing, optometry, and allied health, and college of arts and sciences. Having achieved occupational diversity, the city has finally laid to rest the old adage that "hard times come to Birmingham first and stay longest."

The modern spirit of Birmingham is also attributable to a less tangible element than a healthy economy or educational growth. C. Vann Woodward, the most penetrating scholar of the New South, remarked in 1960 that the southern region was set apart from the rest of the nation by its unique experiences with widespread poverty, military defeat, and a burden of guilt over slavery and its consequences.[58] The South no longer carries these burdens alone. The entire nation is struggling with the problems of poverty and has experienced the frustration of military defeat. Other regions have been forced to confess their own *mea culpa* in matters of race. But Birmingham—the heavy weight of racial injustice at last lifted from its conscience—has a new lightness of the heart.

58. C. Vann Woodward, *The Burden of Southern History* (Baton Rouge: Louisiana State University Press, 1960; New York: Vintage Books, Alfred A. Knopf, 1960), pp. 1–25.

4

Other Voices,
Other Cultures

*F*OR some one hundred centuries, humans have inhabited the land now called Alabama. Primitive food grinding tools and stone points found in Russell Cave in northeastern Alabama attest that prehistoric men and women sought shelter in this huge, dry cavity eight to ten thousand years ago. Pottery fashioned from clay and vegetable fibers some four thousand years ago has been discovered along the Tennessee River. Burial mounds at Moundville, one of the three great temple-mound centers of the Southeast, were built around A.D. 1200. Before the coming of Columbus, Iroquoian Indians (later known as Cherokees) and Muskogean Indians (later called Choctaws, Chickasaws, and Creeks) roamed the hill country and coastal plain. Early European explorers found their descendants pursuing the wild game and tilling the soil of this vast woodland.

The white intruders viewed some aspects of Indian culture with approval. Southeastern Indians lived in simple shelters within towns and farmed for subsistence. Each town was governed by chieftains, one for war and one for civil matters, who gathered occasionally in loose federations to discuss larger matters. Civil war was virtually unknown and civil disputes usually settled by arbitration. Murder was abnormal. Indians practiced burning at the stake in about the same ratio that whites practiced lynching.

But other elements of this native culture were alien to the concepts prevalent among Europeans. Southern Indians were economic communists, insisting that their lands belonged to the tribe as a whole although an individual might own a dog, a horse, clothing, a house, and implements. The tribe planted and harvested communally, each family raising enough to feed its members and to place a portion in a common storehouse for emergencies. Women, although primarily responsible for farming and household chores, were esteemed to a degree which their European sisters might well have envied. Men, having no temptation to acquire wealth, enjoyed leisure to lounge in the sun, joke, gamble, and play games. Opinions of the elderly were heard with respect. Religion was private, nonmissionary, and wholly unrelated to morality, which derived from tribal custom.

Until white men introduced them to the monetary value of pelts and furs, these Indians hunted for subsistence but seldom for sport, killing with bow and arrow (rarely assisted by dogs) only what was needed for food. Hunting grounds being broad, game plentiful, and economic interests virtually nonexistent, southern Indians "no more considered war a sport than they considered hunting a pastime." [1] Tribes exchanged ceremonial visits and engaged in intertribal ball games, meeting one another more often in amity than in war.

This forest culture was altered substantially by the coming of Europeans and Americans. Some Indians adopted the dress of whites, spoke their language (including their profanity), and acquired a taste for creature comforts such as furniture and utensils. As Indian hunting grounds shrank and game became scarce, they turned more assiduously to agriculture. Some prosperous Indians in the Black Belt owned black slaves, tilled large farms, raised livestock, and sent their children to eastern col-

---

1. R.S. Cotterill, *The Southern Indians: The Story of The Civilized Tribes before Removal* (Norman: University of Oklahoma Press, 1954), p. 11.

leges. Cherokees modelled their written constitution after that of the United States.

In other respects, however, Indians stubbornly resisted acculturation. Most full bloods refused to accept the white man's religion or his idea of private land ownership. Southern Indians were as strongly communistic in 1825 as they had been fifty years earlier, considering common ownership of the land an evidence of the unity of the tribe and private ownership a sign of its disintegration. When Indian attachment to the land collided with the constant, unrelenting expansionism of whites, the long process of eradication and removal began.

The first important engagement between European whites and American Indians in what is now the United States took place in 1540 on Alabama soil when the conquistador Hernando de Soto and 950 musket-bearing, armored Spaniards slaughtered the last of the mound builders at the Indian village of Mabila somewhere in present-day Clarke County. Estimates of the number of Indians killed at Mabila range from 2,500 to 11,000.

Although Soto moved on in his quest for gold, the whites who began to come two centuries later planted forts and settlements. French and British courted the Indians to win friendship and trade, Spanish involved them in international intrigues, but Americans trespassed upon their land to hunt, fish, pasture stock, cut timber, and cultivate fields.

In response, militant "Red Sticks" of the Creek confederacy, munitioned by the Spanish, fell upon American settlers in the Alabama-Tombigbee basin in the summer of 1813. At Fort Mims, a rough stockade north of Mobile, "Red Sticks" massacred some 240 men, women, and children. The brief Creek War came to a climax the following February when Andrew Jackson and two thousand followers trapped some one thousand warriors in the horseshoe bend of the Tallapoosa River, virtually annihilated them, and broke Creek resistance.

As punishment for their revolt, the Creeks were forced to surrender most of their Alabama domain. Bowing to the seemingly inevitable, Choctaws, Chickasaws, and Cherokees signed treaties ceding their lands. By 1839 the Indians had bartered their ancestral realm for the plains of Oklahoma and, like the buffalo which once roamed Alabama, had been pushed west of the Mississippi. Bidding farewell, Chief Eufaula of the Creeks told members of the Alabama legislature "the Indian fires are going out" and magnanimously wished them "peace and happiness in the country which my forefathers owned." [2]

Confronted by more complex and materialistic people, Indians vanished from Alabama culturally as well as physically. They left behind their mellifluous place-names (for example, Tuscaloosa, Tallapoosa, Coosa, Cahaba, Talladega, Tallassee, Alabama), their eating habits (peanuts, squash, peppers, tomatoes, pumpkins, and the omnipresent corn), and a smattering of words (among them hominy, succotash, skunk, chipmunk, opossum, raccoon, pecan, hickory).

In the 1970 census 2,443 persons in Alabama identified themselves as American Indians. Some 20 percent of these were clustered around the little community of Poarch near Atmore in Escambia County. Legend has it that these are descendants of Creeks who remained friendly to Americans during the war of 1813–1814 and that this community grew out of a tract of land given to Lynn McGhee, an Indian guide, for his services to Jackson.

Isolated for many years in these swampy flatlands, the friendly Creeks lived much the same agrarian existence as had their forefathers. In the early 1900s they began to work for wages in timbering or agriculture, adopted Episcopalian or Holiness faiths, but were excluded from white schools. When word of the Indians Claims Commission reached Escambia County in the 1950s, however, it suddenly became fashionable to claim Indian descent. According to a local joke, "there used to be three races of people around here; white, Indian, and colored; now there's only two, Indian and colored." [3]

Although Poarch is only a few miles from the busy freeway

2. Moore, *History of Alabama,* p. 32.

3. J. Anthony Paredes, "The Emergence of Contemporary Eastern Creek Indian Identity," *Social and Cultural Identity,* Southern Anthropological Society Proceedings, No. 8 (Athens: University of Georgia Press, 1974), p. 72.

between Montgomery and Mobile, its residents seem far removed from the American mainstream. Their small houses are scattered in haphazard disarray across this lowland. Several Pentecostal churches, a simple frame building marked "community center," the name McGhee on a few mailboxes, and some coffee-skinned children playing in the middle of Route 21 identify the last stand of the Creeks in Alabama. Scruffy ponies browse in bare yards and hogs root in the damp earth. Beside one house is a tattered tent camper. (Do Indians now go camping in tepees on wheels?) Except for the neat brick home of the chief, this is an unkempt community stamped with the impress of poverty.

Led by a descendant of Lynn McGhee, the Indians of Poarch have recently shown an interest in their heritage as well as in their land claims. They have revived the dances, costumes, and powwows of old and even dream of a cultural center on nearby I–65. But it is painfully apparent that this dream will not become reality unless the federal government provides funds and also trains these Creeks in their ancestral crafts. The Indian fires in Alabama may not be totally extinguished but they are flickering only faintly.

To compare Mobile with her sister cities in Alabama is to liken a full-blown, worldly Creole courtesan to a group of prim, Anglo-Saxon girls. Perhaps the prevailing breezes from the sea helped to melt the ice of Puritanism as it seeped down from the north. Mobile's spirited Latin ancestors surely did their part. Maturity also sets Mobile apart. Her name had been on world maps for a century before John Hunt built his cabin by the Big Spring in future Huntsville. At the time of the founding of Montgomery, Mobile had already passed through French, British, and Spanish hands, been a prize in three wars, captured once by the Spanish, and finally by the Americans.

Her strategic location accounted for Mobile's wartorn history. She sprawls along the western shore of a magnificent bay, guarded from the Gulf of Mexico by a barrier island and the long spit of Alabama's eastern shore. She occupies the terminus of a great watershed where six rivers (the Tombigbee, Black

Warrior, Alabama, Cahaba, Coosa, and Tallapoosa) come together to seek the sea.

Unless one accepts the romantic legend that Prince Madoc and fellow Welshmen put ashore in this area during the twelfth century, venturesome Spaniards were the first identifiable whites to discover this bay (although Martin Waldsccmüller's map of 1507 shows the bay). Only twenty-seven years after the first voyage of Columbus, Admiral Alonso Alvárez de Pinĕda probed this body of water and christened it "Bahia de Spiritu Santo." It has since acquired the secular but more prosaic name of Mobile Bay. Pánfilo de Narváez and Alvar Nunez Cabeza de Vaca halted here briefly in 1528. Hernando de Soto passed north of the bay in 1540 after destroying the village of Mabila, leaving little to memorialize these Indians except their name. In 1559 Don Tristán de Luna made an unsuccessful effort to found a Spanish colony on the Gulf Coast, perhaps in the Mobile area.

Frenchmen planted the first permanent colony at Mobile in 1711 after abandoning an earlier settlement within the flood plain of the Mobile River. The French Canadian brothers, Pierre le Moyne, Sieur d'Iberville and Jean Baptiste le Moyne, Sieur de Bienville, were seeking to further the ambition of France to control the Mississippi River basin. Until 1720 the little village which they founded held the eminent title of capital of the vast French province of Louisiana which extended from the Gulf of Mexico into Canada and westward to the Rocky Mountains. Superseded by New Orleans, Mobile was demoted to a mere district capital of this French empire.

In the momentous territorial swaps of the Treaty of Paris of 1763, France ceded its territory east of the Mississippi, including Mobile, to England but reserved western Louisiana and New Orleans for its ally Spain. Although England had failed to win the city which commanded the exit of the Mississippi, she gained at Mobile a bay which could easily have accommodated her entire navy.

At the start of the American Revolution, agents of the Continental Congress distributed copies of the Declaration of Independence in Mobile. But Mobilians, fearful of the Spanish at New Orleans, tied to Britain through trade, and seeing nothing to be gained from revolution, remained overwhelmingly Tory. Their anxiety about the Spanish proved well-founded. In 1780 Spanish forces under Don Bernardo de Gálvez, governor of Louisiana, invaded the bay which Pinēda had circled 260 years earlier and forced the surrender of Fort Charlotte. Mobile remained in Spanish hands for thirty-three years.

In April 1813, Gen. James Wilkinson and 600 Americans surprised a garrison of sixty Spaniards and claimed Mobile for the United States. When it became part of the United States, Mobile was a small but cosmopolitan outpost on the fringe of the rural South, her 300 residents more oriented to trade than to agriculture, more closely tied to the sea than to the hinterland.

Although finally an American city, Mobile retained her strong Latin flavor throughout the antebellum era. As late as the 1850s Philip Gosse noted "a certain something of a foreign appearance." [4] The British visitor attributed this to unfamiliar trees and plants such as the China tree, Adam's needle, honey locusts, magnolias, fan palms, and thickets of prickly pears. This observant naturalist appears to have seen no sign of a luxuriant Oriental flower transplanted by French settlers to the Gulf Coast where it was to blossom so profusely that twentieth-century Mobile would proclaim itself "azalea capital of the world."

Other travellers found Mobile distinctive by reason of a joyous, unbounded appetite for food and drink. The British writer Thomas Hamilton took care to lay in a store of cognac and Scotch biscuits at cosmopolitan Mobile before embarking on a river steamer in 1831 for provincial Montgomery. Another Englishman, James S. Buckingham, remarked upon how openly these southerners partook of strong drink. Grog shops occupied almost every major street corner of Mobile in 1839. Thus tempted, many Mobilians exhibited rowdyism, particularly on election days. When a new Mobile mayor was to be chosen in 1839, sedate residents warned Buckingham that he would encounter five hundred drunk voters before noon and at least one thousand by sunset.

Fondness for spiritous beverages was not confined to the

4. Gosse, *Letters from Alabama,* pp. 25–29.

lower elements of society. Despite the frowns of Mobile's Total Abstinence Society, its early newspapers advertised rum from Jamaica, wine from the islands of Madeira and Teneriffe, whiskey from Ireland, gin from Holland, and a tempting variety of brandies from other far-off ports. Hotels, restaurants, and resorts vied to serve the most exotic liquors. During one of Mobile's periodic yellow fever epidemics prudent citizens were cautioned to fortify their water with claret and, at the first sign of fever, to quaff mint juleps "until the tone of his system raises him above his pains and his fears." (If measures like these failed to effect a cure, the sufferer was advised to "repent of his sins . . . and set about the last arrangement of his worldly concerns.") [5]

Such indulgence perhaps contributed to the popularity of all-night "coffee-saloons" like the Indian Queen on Government Street which served coffee, cakes, and pies to steamboat workers. Festorazzi's, which opened its doors on Royal Street between Dauphin and Conti after the Civil War, became a Mobile version of an old London coffeehouse. Business and political leaders met regularly around its little marble-topped tables to gossip over coffee, made from freshly parched green coffee beans, or a glass of milk accompanied by a spoon for use in dunking one of Capt. Silvester Festorazzi's famous pastries.

More Latin than Puritan in temperament, most Mobilians were free from concern that dancing might be an invention of the devil. In 1835 the English traveller George Featherstonhaugh came upon a group of joyous Spanish Creoles performing the bolero in broad daylight. The British actor Tyrone Power remarked that Mobile society in the 1830s was a mixture of elegance and democracy. At a fashionable ball he observed that the merchant's lady danced in the same set with the *modiste* who had made her costly ballgown, while the merchant himself whirled the wife of his drayman. Despite such egalitarianism, high society in Mobile matched that of Charleston or Savannah in style and manners although its leaders were more likely to be

5. Paul Wayne Taylor, "Mobile: 1818–1859: As Her Newspapers Pictured Her" (master's thesis: University of Alabama, Tuscaloosa, 1951).

merchants than planters. These wealthy Mobilians, an observer commented, dominated their community much as merchant princes had ruled ancient Genoa.

Horseracing, cockfighting, regattas, and an occasional Spanish "bull bait" also diverted antebellum Mobilians from the cares of trade and commerce. A touring stock company made its headquarters in this "city of commerce and liberality." Tyrone Power, performing on a Mobile stage in the 1830s, was upset when some members of his audience exhibited a tendency not uncommon on the nearby frontier. During his performance, the actor noticed a slight scuffle in one of the upper boxes; he later learned that a member of the audience had been efficiently knifed to death and his killers had made their escape, all this causing no more than a ripple of disturbance.

Members of polite society might encounter ruffians at a public theater or deign to dance with simpler folk at a ball but carefully restricted those invited to their private homes or weddings. The custom of holding open house on New Year's Day was observed in Mobile for years. Men in full evening dress made the rounds of fashionable homes where hostesses plied them with food and drink. Women took their turn at visiting on weekday afternoons when hostesses on appointed streets were "at home."

Madame Octavia Walton Le Vert was the undisputed queen of Mobile's antebellum society. For a quarter of a century she reigned over a salon in the drawing room of her Government Street home. Ambassadors, politicians, artists, and virtually every visiting dignitary called upon Madame Le Vert, attracted by her reputation as a beauty, a wit, and a linguist. When Madame Le Vert left Mobile after the Civil War, she was succeeded as its social leader by the more reserved Augusta Evans Wilson, author of *St. Elmo, Beulah,* and other best sellers of the mid-nineteenth century.

In the decade before Mobile became an object of conquest in a fourth war, its 20,500 inhabitants constituted Alabama's largest urban center, outranking both Montgomery and Huntsville. This growth had come about through the trading of cotton rather than its cultivation. Numerous commission merchants (called "factors"), who acted as intermediaries between planters and the markets of the eastern United States and Europe, made Mobile their headquarters. The Alabama and Tombigbee rivers were the lifelines of this interchange. From the 1820s into the early twentieth century, steamboats plied between Mobile and river ports like Selma, Montgomery, Demopolis, and Gainesville, providing the chief means of exodus for the planters and cotton of the Black Belt. George Featherstonhaugh observed thirty to forty three-masted schooners riding at anchor in Mobile Bay in 1835, ready to load cotton and passengers for Liverpool, London, or Le Havre.

Being a seaport and commercial center, Mobile attracted a more polyglot population than other Alabama cities. In addition to the Creole community clustered around Chastang's Bluff, it received an invigorating influx of immigrants from Germany, Sweden, England, Ireland, and other northern European countries as well as numerous Yankees and vagrant sailors from over the world. Sixty-three percent of the foreign-born residents of Alabama during the 1850s lived in Mobile. As late as the 1880s a reporter for *Harper's Weekly* judged the population of Mobile to be more varied in nationality and descent than that of any other city in the United States. Mobilians combined a love of spicy repartee and an ability to laugh at themselves, both derived from their French ancestry, with an egalitarianism more like that of an eastern than a southern city.

Its black population was also unusual in that around one thousand free blacks, almost one-half of Alabama's total free black population in 1860, lived in Mobile County. Many of these were descendants of free blacks admitted to citizenship under terms of the treaty by which Spain had transferred this portion of West Florida to the United States. During the 1850s every free black in Mobile was required to report to the city's mayor each year and post bond to keep the peace and maintain good behavior for the ensuing year.

Cotton trading and afternoons "at home" were rudely interrupted by Civil War. While the Union's Adm. David Farragut guarded the exit of Mobile Bay against all but the most daring privateers, the Confederacy's Adm. Raphael Semmes and his raider *Alabama* were wreaking havoc upon Union shipping in the Atlantic. Semmes, a Marylander by birth but a Mobile lawyer by choice, guided his cruiser on a two-year spree during which she sank fifty-seven ships and captured many more before being sunk by the *Kearsage*. (Semmes escaped and hurried back to Confederate service.)

Shortly after news of the loss of the *Alabama* reached Mobile, her citizens were further alarmed by the prospect that Farragut and his ships would run the gauntlet between Forts Morgan and Gaines at the entrance to their bay. As the fiercest naval battle of the Civil War began on August 5, 1864, all but one of eighteen Union gunboats passed safely into the bay. When his lead ship, the *Tecumseh,* exploded and sank, Farragut realized that the channel was mined with torpedoes. Faced with the decision between retreat and possible destruction of his fleet, the Union admiral issued his classic command, "Damn the torpedos: Full speed ahead!" Union ships soon knocked three small Confederate gunboats out of the battle but the ironclad *Tennessee* matched her six guns and 200 men against seventeen ships, 199 guns, and seven hundred Federals for three hours before surrendering. Mobile's citizens barricaded their city, stacked cotton bales in Bienville Square, and held out until after Appomattox, becoming the last coastal city in the Confederacy to fall.

Visiting Mobile in the spring of 1865, the reporter Whitelaw Reid noticed some of Farragut's fleet still anchored off the tumbled wharves and empty warehouses of Mobile's harbor. But when Reid returned the following November, torpedoes had been removed from the bay, new warehouses were rising, and a fleet of sail and steam vessels lined the repaired wharves. Cotton trading had resumed and Mobile bustled with "the new blood of the South." She continued to dredge her channel and enlarge her docks until in 1976 thirty-three ocean-going vessels of forty-foot draught could be accommodated simultaneously.

Although modern Mobile exports more timber, iron, and steel products than cotton, she has not lost sight of her old French and Spanish heritage. Mobile's citizens still celebrate the oldest Mardi Gras revels in the New World, predating those of their longtime rival New Orleans. As early as 1830 masked members of Mobile's Cowbellian de Rakin Society paraded, danced, and feasted on New Year's Eve. The Cowbellians were succeeded in 1841 by the Striker's Club whose members travelled en masse to New Orleans the following year to attend the first ball of that city's Mystic Krewe of Comus. Mardi Gras in New Orleans has since outstripped that of Mobile in size and national attention. Mobilians have a ready explanation for this: they claim that the citizens of New Orleans parade for tourists while they cavort for their own amusement.

Mobile cherishes other reminders of her past. Although her original French and Spanish dwellings were destroyed by fire more than a century ago, copies of these Creole cottages, raised above the humid earth, are plentiful. Town houses garnished with iron lace outnumber Greek Revival temples. Mobile wantonly defied Prohibition during the 1920s and dared to erect Alabama's first dogracing track in the 1960s. Its citizens continue to indulge a lusty appetite and quench a boundless thirst. Sober-minded hinterlanders, drawn to Mobile for conventions, experience a strange giddiness at the sight of such open and unashamed self-indulgence. Mobile's blithe Mediterranean spirit still lifts the heart and tempts the flesh.

Alabama has suffered the loss of her natural coastline to a greater degree than any other seaboard state. That narrow ribbon of sand and pine barrens between the Perdido and Apalachicola rivers should have been part of Alabama. It is the watershed through which eight Alabama rivers flow to the sea. Its climate and terrain resemble those of interior Alabama. Its early history was more closely tied to Alabama than to the peninsula. Indians and Spanish traders moved freely up and down these river routes. Alabamians and West Floridians mingled frequently in fighting units of the Confederacy. Southeastern Alabama traded with Pensacola and other coastal ports. But in the process of wars and treaties, Florida got a Panhandle which East Floridians originally regarded as a nuisance, and Alabama lost a seacoast beloved by generations of her citizens.

After Spain renounced all claim to West Florida in 1819 and

ceded the eastern peninsula to the United States, considerable sentiment favored annexing the northwestern seacoast to Alabama. Floridians, having been divided under both Spanish and British rule, were accustomed to the idea of two Floridas. Residents of Florida's east and west sections were political rivals. As early as 1821 the Alabama legislature urged its congressional delegation to seek annexation. On eight other occasions over a period of 150 years, Alabama expressed this recurring desire although jealous Mobilians evidenced little enthusiasm at the prospect of admitting the port of Pensacola. When serious negotiations began in 1868, Florida's commissioners actually expressed willingness to cede ten thousand miles of their coast to Alabama in return for $1 million in thirty-year, 8-percent bonds. East Floridians often seemed anxious to rid themselves of the Panhandle. West Floridians, although divided, generally favored the change. But opposition to the purchase rose in western Alabama and Mobile. Opponents argued that the price was too high for a "sand bank and gopher region" and that Alabamians could use the Pensacola harbor without buying the Panhandle. Floridians began to have second thoughts about ceding such an excellent harbor. All nine annexation movements failed and two-thirds of southern Alabama remained permanently landlocked.[6]

To look on the brighter side, perhaps Alabama should consider herself fortunate to have wrested Mobile from Mississippi. When the Mississippi Territory was being divided by Congress into two states, it appeared for a time that the Tombigbee River might become the boundary, thereby locating Mobile within Mississippi. Fortunately for Alabama, she retained Mobile and a coastal fringe of some seventy miles on either side of the bay.

Alabama's truncated coast lies mostly within one county, larger in size than Rhode Island and only slightly smaller than Delaware. Baldwin County produces more diverse crops and shelters a more heterogeneous population than any other rural

6. The tangled negotiations for this coastline are traced by Jerrell H. Shofner, "The Chimerical Scheme of Ceding West Forida," *Alabama Historical Quarterly* 33 (Spring 1971): 5–36.

area of Alabama. Its seacoast, its climate which permits at least two crops a year, and its abundant and once-cheap land have drawn numerous colonies of outlanders to Baldwin.

Connecticut Yankees led by Josiah Blakeley founded a bustling port on the eastern shore of Mobile after the War of 1812. Blakeley resembled a New England seaport in its federal architecture and enterprising spirit. Within a decade it had outdistanced Mobile in population and as a shipping point for cotton, lumber, and locally-distilled whiskey. Yellow fever, wild land speculation, and the silting of its harbor reduced Blakeley to a ghost town by 1836, but it was destined to reappear in history for a brief moment. Confederates and Yankees fought one of the last battles of the Civil War (three days after Appomattox) near its ruins.

Having discovered the benign climate of Baldwin County, some Union soldiers returned to farm and live in amity among their former enemies. Other immigrants, wooed by lumber companies with no further use for land which they had stripped of timber, were attracted to Baldwin. A group of Italians came in the late 1880s to plant rice, tobacco, potatoes, truck crops and even vineyards on onetime cotton land near a little community they called Daphne. Scandinavians (at Silverhill), Greeks (at Malbis), Germans, Poles, Czechs, French Canadians, American Quakers, and Hooker Mennonites later joined in transforming the devastated forests to fertile fields.

Soybeans are a major enterprise today along with potatoes, truck crops, gladioli, pecans, livestock, and commercial fishing. Oysters have been harvested by the fleet of the little village of Bon Secour ("Safe Harbor") for more than a hundred years. (It is said that oldtimers in Bon Secour, lying abed on still nights, can identify each fishing boat which passes up or down their river by the sound of its engine.)

One Baldwin County enclave differs markedly from these fishing and farming communities. Point Clear on the bay across from Mobile has been a fashionable watering place for southerners since the 1830s. Planters and genteel families from Louisiana, Mississippi, and Georgia as well as Alabama came to

Point Clear in the antebellum era to sail, dance, gamble, and introduce younger generations to suitable mates. The Civil War interrupted these idyllic pastimes. "Dearest," wrote a young southern swain in 1860, "I fear I shall not see you at Point Clear this summer. I am leaving this evening for Vicksburg." [7] Admiral Farragut had the effrontery to bombard Point Clear in 1864, leaving the mark of a Yankee cannonball for future generations of southerners to ponder.

Point Clear is still a plush resort but it attracts a more democratic clientele now. The more affluent come in winter, southerners often mixing congenially with Yankees. These southern patrons are prone to subject strangers to a brief and unabashed inquisition: "Where are you from?" "What's your business?" "Where'd you go to college?" "What's your fraternity?" "What church do you attend?" This is not mere idle curiosity. The answers serve to identify a stranger's rank within the social and economic hierarchy of the South, often proving fruitful in discovering remote cousins, sorority sisters, or fellow Episcopalians. Observing this process at work, Carl Carmer remarked that it sometimes seemed to him as if the entire state of Alabama were bound into one family. (There is a lot of truth to this observation except that this "family" is comprised exclusively of whites of comfortable income.)

In the evenings Point Clear exudes conviviality. The capacious dining room of Grand Hotel abounds in chatter, good cheer, and the bustle of serving an abundance of food and drink. A noisy band adds to the merriment, attracting some unusual couples to the dance floor: fathers with their nubile daughters, mothers with their teen-aged sons, grandmothers guided by small boys, all these elders busily inculcating the old southern graces in their young.

During hotter and less fashionable seasons, Point Clear is taken over by middle-level executives and their families from nearby Mississippi or inland Alabama. These natives are un-

7. Hodding Carter and Anthony Ragusin, *Gulf Coast Country*, American Folkways Series (New York: Duell Sloan and Pearce, 1951), pp. 220–221.

daunted by the humidity and attack the golf course with a resolution worthy of old Farragut himself: "Damn the mosquitos
. . . etc."

Close by this colony of the well-to-do is the oldest and largest single-tax experiment in America. Fairhope was founded shortly after the great panic of 1893 by a group of Iowans determined to prove the soundness of the theory argued by Henry George in *Progress and Poverty*. These single-taxers believe that land should be socialized because its supply is fixed by nature and cannot be increased. They do not advocate total socialization however, contending that individuals are entitled to the profits which they make from farming, business, or industry.

The Fairhope Single Tax Corporation, incorporated under Alabama law in 1904, continues to lease land in return for a rent (single tax) based on a valuation of the land which is reassessed annually. Rents are used to pay all county, state, and land taxes, and to improve community services such as streets, parks, a library, water system, and electric plant. Single taxers and "nonbelievers" live side by side in Fairhope but the corporation will only lease to dedicated proponents of its theory.[8]

In the early 1900s an innovative Minnesota schoolteacher convinced the corporation to lease a parcel of land for an experiment in progressive education. The Fairhope School of Organic Education was years ahead of its time in practicing the concept that children should be freed from the strictures of grades and promotion to express their creativity. The school, like the corporation, still exists.

In the tolerant atmosphere of the seacoast, the wealthy, the semisocialistic, the Yankee, and the foreign-born have coexisted in harmony. Alabamians (when they are not expending their vacation dollars in the Florida Panhandle) come from the hinterlands to Baldwin County to taste of exotic foods (gumbos, court bouillon, West Indies salad, oyster loaf, pralines, hush puppies, shrimp jambalaya), to drink beer or more potent bever-

---

8. For a detailed study of the Fairhope experiment see Paul E. and Blanche R. Alyea, *Fairhope, 1894–1954: The Story of a Single-Tax Colony* (University, Ala.: University of Alabama Press, 1956).

ages openly and unashamed, to pursue the big fish or simply to doze in the midday sun, the relentless inner Puritan momentarily giving way to the pagan Celt under the spell of the sea and to the ghostly applause of the old Creoles.

Cajuns are set apart from their fellow Alabamians by the mystery which beclouds their racial heritage. These are not descendants of the peaceful, French-speaking, Roman Catholic farmers expelled from Nova Scotia in 1755 to drift into other colonies, particularly into French Louisiana. They do not conform to the meaning of the term *Creole* when used to denote a person of European descent born in the Americas. Alabama's Cajuns may be a mixture of Anglo-Saxons, French, Spanish, Choctaws, and Apaches but suspicion persists that this mélange also contains a faint trace of African ancestry. To be called Cajun in Alabama therefore is a stigma rather than a source of ethnic pride.

No one knows for certain how many Cajuns still inhabit the remote piney woods of upper Mobile or lower Washington counties around Mount Vernon and Citronelle. The most common guess is that they number around three thousand. But some facts about these Cajuns have been painfully obvious to the few observers who have taken any interest in them since World War II. They found the majority to be poorly educated, malnourished, existing at or near the poverty level, and afflicted by ulcers, high blood pressure, venereal diseases, and a hyperventilation syndrome.

Their speech and accent betray a mixed cultural background, blending archaic expressions of the southern mountains with words of French origin. Perhaps because of their isolation, Cajuns preserve much of the vernacular of Alabama's early Scotch-Irish settlers. They say "proud" for glad, a "sight" for much, "carry" for accompany, "chunk" for throw, "smart" for industrious, and "tote" for haul. An envelope is "backed" instead of addressed, double words (biscuit-bread, women-folks, church-house) and plurals ("ghosties," "nestes," "folk-sies") are common. "Evening" begins at noon. Yet this Anglo-Saxon dialect is sprinkled with French and Creole usages such as "gallery" for porch, "bayou" for a body of water, "filé" for sassafras. Their eating habits also reflect a hybrid inheritance: Indian dishes like succotash and gumbo filé, a French affinity for dripped coffee made from parched green coffee beans, a taste for exotic dishes such as green turtle meat and barbecued goat.[9]

It is not their picturesque speech, their unusual foods, or their Indian and French antecedents which have set the Cajuns apart but the persistent whisper that some of them are descended from Daniel Reed, a free black from the Caribbean islands, and his wife Rose, a mulatto slave owned by Young Gaines, a member of a family which held large tracts of land in the Alabama territory. Daniel Reed, it is reported, purchased Rose and his eight children from Gaines. Over the ensuing decades, these children and their descendants interbred with whites, Choctaws, and perhaps with the Apache Indians who, along with their leader Geronimo, were briefly relocated during the 1880s at Fort Stoddard thirty miles north of Mobile. No matter if the blood of Daniel and Rose Reed had been diluted by many another racial strain, an Alabama judge decreed in the early 1940s that the Cajun children involved in one suit were one-sixty-fourth black and therefore not eligible to attend white schools.

Since then some young Cajuns have escaped segregation to attend high schools in the Mobile area and others have been integrated into neighborhood schools. But an observer in 1967 found numbers of young Cajuns still lumped into one substandard school. When these pupils emerged for recess, he noted the variety of their appearance: blond children with kinky hair; dark children with straight hair; others with red hair, freckles, and a hint of Africa, or Indian cheekbones below Teutonic blue eyes.[10]

Some Alabama Cajuns have managed to find jobs in nearby chemical plants and shipyards and these bring home at least the

9. Laura Frances Murphy, "The Cajans at Home," *Alabama Historical Quarterly* 2 (Winter 1940): 416–427.

10. Richard Severo, "The Lost Tribe of Alabama," *Scanlan's* 1 (March 1970): 81–88.

minimum weekly wage. Still they are unable to escape persecution by those who hold them racially suspect. Cajuns themselves are racists, violently resentful of blacks. In turn, most blacks avoid them because, as one explained: "They ain't white and they ain't black. They ain't nothin'." [11] To be people without a racial identity in Alabama still poses many dilemmas; pride in their cosmopolitan ethnic background has yet to be instilled in the Cajuns of Mobile and Washington counties.

Three groups of colonists were drawn to Alabama during the nineteenth century by the "vineyard dream," an idyllic but ill-fated notion of reproducing the European wine industry in the American South. One colony found the climate unsuitable and the work too demanding; another foundered in heavy financial seas, and a third encountered sterile soil and hostile prohibitionists. Thus there is no replica of France's Moselle Valley in subtropical Alabama today; wine is imported from California, New York, and abroad, or made by amateurs for their own amusement.

The first, most glamorous, and most incongruous of these vineyard colonies was comprised of military officers and political leaders of the fallen empire of Napoleon I. When their emperor was imprisoned on remote Saint Helena after Waterloo, these Frenchmen and their wives sought refuge and a new way of life in the United States. Congress in 1817 agreed to the sale of four townships in the Alabama wilderness, at two dollars per acre to be repaid over fourteen years, upon condition that the 340 allottees would devote themselves to the peaceful occupation of cultivating the vine and olive. The émigrés selected a site near the confluence of the Warrior and Tombigbee rivers because its chalky fertile land and high river bluffs reminded them of the faraway valleys of the Somme and the Seine.[12]

The gale which almost swamped their schooner as it ap-

---

11. Severo, "Lost Tribe of Alabama," p. 88.

12. For a chapter on the Vine and Olive Colony, see Albert James Pickett, *History of Alabama* (1878; reprint ed.: Birmingham: Birmingham Book and Magazine Co., 1962), pp. 623–634.

proached Mobile Bay was an omen of troubles to come. The colonists boarded a barge for an unknown land which they were to share with Choctaws and a smattering of white pioneers. They erected cabins on a white bluff near the juncture of the rivers (unaware that this site lay outside their grant), gave Demopolis its democratic name ("city of the people"), and confronted the awesome task of clearing thick stands of cane from this forest.

Perhaps the root cause of their failure was nature herself. Grapes ripened in the heat of summer and turned to vinegar before they fermented. Frosts withered hundreds of olive trees. New vines and seeds arrived from Bordeaux too late for planting. German redemptioners failed in their half-hearted efforts to clear the cane; it would require gangs of slaves, often driven by the whip, to accomplish this task.

Refined Frenchmen and their ladies, accustomed to the comforts of Paris, lacked the toughness to conquer a frontier. Nothing in their experience at the Battles of Saragossa, Bordeaux, or Waterloo had prepared them for this struggle. Neither their acquaintance with history and philosophy nor their gifts in music, poetry, and conversation sustained them against attacks by strange fevers, venomous insects, and land thieves who poached upon their preserve. Gradually they retreated, some to Mobile, others to France, relinquishing their vineyards to the cotton planters, leaving only a few olive trees and a touch of Gallic legendry to mark their sojourn in the Black Belt.

Did Count LeFebre Desnouettes, the French commander at the siege of Saragossa, and Gen. Juan Rico, his Spanish counterpart at that great clash of arms, actually toast one another in a pioneer cabin near the confluence of the Warrior and the Tombigbee? Was the keeper of the ferry which crossed French Creek near Demopolis really the same Col. Nicholas Raoul who had accompanied Bonaparte on his triumphant progression from Elba to the gates of Paris? Was the tavernkeeper at Greensboro actually Col. J. J. Cluis who had been charged with the custody of King Ferdinand VII when that Spanish monarch was Napoleon's prisoner? Had that handsome woman in a lonely Alabama cabin really been an attendant to Caroline Bonaparte Murat, sister of Napoleon, when Marshal Joachim Murat had reigned as king of Naples? Did such unlikely pioneers really attempt to grow grapes and olive trees in the Alabama wilderness? Or was it only a dream?

Across the state from Demopolis, other vineyards blossomed briefly, only to be forgotten even more completely than the French experiment. Northern entrepreneurs in the 1890s envisioned transforming a portion of Alabama's piney woods into a winemaking region. They selected an elevated site near the Georgia border which had required such extensive grading by the Southern Railway that it was originally called "Summit Cut." Scotch-Irish farm families chose the more euphonic name of Zidonia (pronouncing it "Zidonee") but proved willing to move to Sand Mountain when northern speculators offered to buy their lands. The Alabama Fruit Growers and Winery Association awarded $25 to a woman who proposed the new name of Fruithurst, connoting cultivation of the intended crops in a wooded grove.[13]

This experiment attracted people of Swedish, Danish, and Norwegian extraction who established small business enterprises and labored in the vineyards and wineries of Fruithurst. Its developers laid out an ambitious "model city" with intricate diagonal streets instead of the usual checkerboard pattern. Compared to the Scotch-Irish names of Alabama's white majority, many surnames in Fruithurst rang strangely on the ear: for example, Hokanson, Keirsala, Hizar, Boalch, and DeGraf. The first child born to members of the colony was christened Lizzie Fruithurst Youda.

During Fruithurst's brief boom, crowds of curious visitors and business representatives were attracted by its advertising and its showplace, the Fruithurst Inn, a Victorian structure with eighty guestrooms, a bowling alley, a billiard room, and a rotunda lobby large enough to accommodate musicales or a full orchestra. The inn was renowned for its cuisine which on

13. Virginia Voss Pope, *Fruithurst: Alabama's Vineyard Village*, ed. Larry Joe Smith (Albertville, Ala.: Thompson Printing Co., 1971) is a small publication devoted to this experiment.

Thanksgiving Day in 1898 included such delicacies as wild goose a la Farmiere, queen of soufflé, sabayon, puree of tomatoes a la Reine, shrimp salad, and Columbia River salmon, all washed down by generous quantities of Fruithurst claret.

Perhaps such elaborate food and entertainment contributed to the bankruptcy that year of the Fruit Growers and Winery Association. After 1898 Fruithurst dwindled steadily. Its two newspapers, the *Weekly Enterprise* and the *Vineyardist,* which published columns devoted to grape cultivation and winemaking, had ceased publication by 1905. Its inn, stores, and Scandinavian populace vanished. In the census of 1970 Fruithurst showed a population of only 229. Orchards and wineries long gone, some of its residents turned to other money-making enterprises, earning their town brief national notoriety in 1975 as a "speed trap" for motorists hurrying between Birmingham and Atlanta.

Unlike Fruithurst and Demopolis, Cullman thrived after abandoning its vineyards. Col. Johann Gottfried Cullman, a Bavarian adventurer who supposedly led a brief insurrection against Prussians during the German Revolution of 1848, founded this haven for his fellow countrymen. Like the Napoleonic exiles, Cullman was a refugee from his native land. Encouraged by the Louisville and Nashville Railroad and by Gov. Robert M. Patton, he wooed settlers to the community of Cullman by advertising in the northern press: "Tracts, 40 acres and up, $2.00–$6.00 per acre. agricultural, timber, iron, coal and minerals. Climate healthful. No malaria, no swamps, no grasshoppers, no hurricanes, and no blizzards." [14] (Also no fertile land, a fact which Colonel Cullman omitted to mention.)

Like the French a half-century earlier, the Germans learned that grapes did not thrive in parts of Alabama, particularly not in the hill country. "The soil was so poor," one reported, "[that] we should not have stayed but we were too poor to leave." [15] Germans deemed cornmeal fit only for livestock but were forced, like earlier pioneers, to subsist on this staple, mo-

14. Jones, *Combing Cullman County,* p. 28.
15. Jones, *Combing Cullman County,* p. 15.

lasses, and potatoes. They learned to cultivate corn, sweet potatoes, and strawberries; started a flour mill, vinegar factory, cigar
factory, and brickyard; and planted flowers, grass, and shrubs
on the lawns of their neat homes, disdaining to sweep the bare
dirt as did their Scotch-Irish neighbors.

For a time Cullman remained a German island surrounded by
a sea of Scotch-Irish. Saloons and a beer garden served local
wines, beer, and cold cuts; brass bands played military tunes
and Old World songs; its citizens danced, spoke German, read
German-language newspapers, and conducted religious services
in their native language. Cullman's sizable Catholic population
attracted Benedictine monks and nuns to found a monastery,
nunnery, and two colleges there in the 1890s.

Prohibition and two world wars erased much of the German
imprint from Cullman. "Drys" marched in its streets as early as
1906; since then Cullman County has fluctuated between the
preferences of its "wet" and "dry" citizens. During these
wars, the Scotch-Irish observed their German-speaking neighbors with such suspicion that residents ceased to worship in
their native tongue and the *Staata Zeitung* stopped publication in
1942. Modern Cullman is virtually indistinguishable from any
other Alabama community of its size save for the replica of Colonel Cullman's Bavarian mansion as the home of its Chamber
of Commerce. Names like Prinz, Meisner, Brodrecht, Dietz,
and Reinschmidt have persisted but Colonel Cullman's winery
and the vineyards have long since disappeared. The resolute
Germans, refusing to admit defeat, traded their grape presses for
chicken brooders, closed their saloons and beer gardens, abandoned German for English, and were amalgamated into Alabama's white majority.

Migration to Alabama reached its high-water mark early in
the nineteenth century, then dwindled to a comparative trickle.
Some "carpetbaggers" remained after the dismantling of Reconstruction. Immigrants from Ireland, England, Scotland, Germany, and Italy found their way this deep into the South to
labor in the coal mines and iron furnaces around Birmingham.
After World War II a team of German scientists led by Dr.

Wernher von Braun worked in Huntsville when Alabama's old capital became a center of rocket and missile construction. These scientists produced at Redstone Arsenal the first American earth satellite, Explorer I, and the Redstone rocket which launched this nation's first astronaut, Alan B. Shepard, Jr., into space.

In the past quarter of a century, numbers of easterners and midwesterners have been dispatched to Alabama to represent large corporations, chains, and industries. Such newcomers, having a skewed image of Alabama, are often reluctant to come. Discovering temperate winters, bounteous lakes and rivers, sizable vestiges of forest, uncrowded spaces, and new racial attitudes, they seem delighted to remain.

*   *   *   *   *

Another recent migration, although still a small one, is a particularly meaningful portent for Alabama and her sister states. A few blacks have begun to return to the South from places such as Michigan, Illinois, and New York to which massive numbers had fled in search of jobs and equal treatment under the law. Unlike their ancestors, these reverse migrants are not being brought South in bondage. They *choose* to return.

A Final Word

*T*HIS essay has focused upon Alabama's white and black majorities, her traditional white elite, and a few atypical cultures. It would be incomplete without mention of another Alabama minority—those who have appeared throughout this state's history on the cutting edge of social, political, or economic progress.

Scholars of the American South have consistently noted this region's characteristic resistance to change and have pondered the reasons for such marked reluctance. W. J. Cash, in his interpretation of southerners, attributed this tendency to a closed state of mind (he called this the "Savage Ideal") which suppressed dissent and enforced conformity. Cash believed that the "Savage Ideal" was rooted in the South's defensive posture on slavery and that it spread later to equate every criticism with disloyalty, "making criticism so dangerous that only a madman would risk it." [1]

Yet the eminent historian C. Vann Woodward holds that this region has not displayed an entirely monolithic mind. His academic colleagues Carl N. Degler and Bruce Clayton have followed Woodward's lead in documenting the presence of southerners who dared to defy the "Savage Ideal" by pointing to

1. Cash, *Mind of the South,* p. 93.

flaws in southern society and who risked ostracism by calling for change.[2]

Over the course of Alabama's history, a number of voices have been raised in support of what Degler has termed "the other South." Almost all suffered in consequence. Some left Alabama rather than pay the price of dissent. Others remained to witness change and the fulfillment of their prophesies. Although a few achieved fame, most have been forgotten by Alabama history. No study of these Alabama dissenters exists. But a few examples will serve to illustrate the presence in Alabama of members of a persistent southern minority.

Early in the great debate over slavery, James G. Birney, a Kentuckian by birth, decided to leave his adopted state of Alabama because he had failed to rally support for the moderate idea of recolonizing blacks in Africa. When Birney attempted to explain his colonization scheme in a series of articles in a Huntsville newspaper, he aroused suspicion and was advised by a friend to temper his words lest he be charged with incendiarism. But Birney foresaw, even in 1833, that the slavery issue, unless resolved, would sever the Union. In two unsuccessful campaigns as the Liberty party's presidential candidate, he sought to avert this catastrophe. When it arrived, those Alabamians who dissented from secession and from the Confederate cause, like Alfred Holley and Chris Sheets, were persecuted, labeled "Tories," and ostracized.

In the bitter aftermath of war and Reconstruction, native white Alabamians who dared to admit their affiliation with the Republican party also became outcasts. The *Montgomery Advertiser* branded them "political lepers." Residents of Tuscaloosa were advised by the *Independent Monitor* that these Republicans were "dogs and should be treated as dogs." It was reported in

---

2. C. Vann Woodward, *The Strange Career of Jim Crow*, 2nd rev. ed. (New York: Oxford University Press, 1966); and *The Burden of Southern History*; Carl N. Degler, *The Other South: Southern Dissenters in the Nineteenth Century* (New York: Harper and Row, 1974); Bruce Clayton, *The Savage Ideal: Intolerance and Intellectual Leadership in the South, 1890–1914* (Baltimore: Johns Hopkins Press, 1972).

Huntsville that many native whites had deserted the Republican party because of persecution.[3]

Others who dissented from the Democratic majority met with hostility and cries of "radical." During the 1890s, Populist followers of Reuben Kolb and Joseph Manning risked social ostracism, loss of credit, even physical attack. Manning, a young Clay County politician, found it hard to explain what led him to advocate such "radical" schemes as a graduated income tax, direct election of United States senators, the secret ballot, a shorter work day for labor, restrictions in immigration, federal warehousing for crops, and a postal savings system. "It was just in me," he said. "I was never a Bourbon Democrat." [4] Disheartened at the failure of his cause, Manning became an exile in New York City.

Yet the need for a two-party system in Alabama and the South appeared obvious to William Garrott Brown, a southern intellectual reared and educated in the small town of Marion. The "politics of uniformity," Brown wrote in 1910, caused the South to be taken for granted by Democrats and ignored by Republicans. Brown castigated the "defeatist attitude" of an Alabama editor who remarked in 1913 that there were not enough Republicans in the state "to hold a state convention in a big hall." But this native Alabama scholar made his comments from afar, finding Harvard University a more hospitable forum for the exchange of ideas. Brown died in 1914, half a century before Republicanism became openly fashionable in Alabama.[5]

Hugo L. Black, like his fellow Clay Countian Joe Manning before him, was called "radical" in the 1920s and 1930s when he advocated government operation of power dams on the Tennessee River, federal health insurance, a permanent Civilian Conservation Corps, federal aid to schools, a forty-hour work week, a minimum wage, and an end to child labor. Aroused op-

3. See Sarah Woolfolk Wiggins, "Ostracism of White Republicans in Alabama During Reconstruction," *Alabama Review* 27 (January 1974): 52–64.

4. Hamilton, *Hugo Black: The Alabama Years,* p. 12.

5. For a study of Brown, see Clayton, *The Savage Ideal.*

ponents predicted that Black would be defeated if he ran for re-election to the United States Senate in 1938. Before this campaign could begin, President Franklin D. Roosevelt appointed the Alabamian to the Supreme Court. In 1954 Justice Black participated in the Court's historic, unanimous decision outlawing segregated education. Many fellow Alabamians angrily called him Judas. Although Justice Black is, in the opinion of many, the most distinguished national figure to emerge from Alabama origins, the shadow of the Savage Ideal still obscures his greatness in his native state.

Race has cast its dark shadow over many another Alabama career in law or politics, including those of James Edwin Horton, Jr., judge at the Scottsboro trials; former Gov. James E. Folsom, an early voice for racial moderation; and United States Fifth District Judge Frank M. Johnson, Jr., who faced up to the responsibility of making many difficult decisions related to racial matters in the 1960s and 1970s. Now that Alabama has taken a fresh direction in racial relations, will the "Savage Ideal" gradually be replaced by open-mindedness?

* * * * *

Degler, the historian of "the other South," has concluded that the ultimate reason for writing any book of history is to assist in escaping the power of the past by understanding it. "Only by consciously knowing one's history," Degler wrote, "can one begin to transcend it." [6] This essay has been written in the hope of furthering that cause.

6. Degler, *The Other South*, p. 9.

Suggestions for Further Reading

Readers who wish to delve more deeply into Alabama history might begin with accounts by antebellum observers such as Frederick Law Olmsted or Joseph Baldwin. Olmsted's comments are available in a paperback edition of *The Cotton Kingdom* (Indianapolis: Bobbs-Merrill Company, Inc., 1971); Baldwin's fictionalized account of early settlement, also in paperback, is *The Flush Times of Alabama and Mississippi* (New York: Hill and Wang, 1957). Philip Gosse, *Letters from Alabama* (London: Morgan and Chase, 1859), a charming account of the flora, fauna, and planter society of the Black Belt, is only available in libraries or private collections.

These personal accounts are evocative of the folk history of the hill country: Mary Gordon Duffee, *Sketches of Alabama,* eds., Virginia Pounds Brown and Jane Porter Nabors (University, Ala.: University of Alabama Press, 1970); Mitchell B. Garrett, *Horse and Buggy Days on Hatchet Creek* (University, Ala.: University of Alabama Press, 1957), and Herman C. Nixon, *Lower Piedmont County,* American Folkways Series (1936: reprint, Freeport, N.Y.: Books for Libraries Press, 1971). Except for the slave narratives, folk history of the Black Belt is largely devoted to romanticized accounts of plantation life from the viewpoint of whites. Amelia M. Gayle Fry, *Memories of Old Cahaba* (Nashville: Printed for the Author, 1908) is a prime example. Autobiographical accounts include Victoria Virginia Clayton, *Black and White Under the Old Regime* (Freeport, N.Y.: Books for Libraries Press, 1970), dealing with the nineteenth century, and Viola Goode Liddell, *With a Southern Accent* (Norman, Okla.: University of Oklahoma Press, 1948), focusing on the early twentieth century.

For readers seriously interested in Alabama politics, these are suggested: Thomas P. Abernethy, *The Formative Period in Alabama, 1815–1828* (University, Ala.: University of Alabama Press, 1965); Allen J. Going, *Bourbon Democracy in Alabama, 1874–1890* (University, Ala.: University of Alabama Press, 1951); William Warren

177

Rogers, *The One-Gallused Rebellion: Agrarianism in Alabama, 1865–1896* (Baton Rouge: Louisiana State University Press, 1970); F. Sheldon Hackney, *Populism to Progressivism in Alabama* (Princeton: Princeton University Press, 1969); Malcolm C. McMillan, *Constitutional Development in Alabama, 1798–1901: A Study in Politics, the Negro, and Sectionalism* (Chapel Hill: University of North Carolina Press, 1955); Virginia V. Hamilton, *Hugo Black: The Alabama Years* (Baton Rouge: Louisiana State University Press, 1972), and William D. Barnard, *Dixiecrats and Democrats, Alabama Politics, 1942–1950* (University, Ala.: University of Alabama Press, 1974).

For race relations, the neglected slave narratives give poignant glimpses of slavery from the viewpoint of blacks: George P. Rawick, ed., *The American Slave: A Composite Autobiography,* vol. 6, *Alabama and Indiana Narratives* (Westport, Conn.: Greenwood Publishing Company, 1972). Scholars who have written responsible accounts of various aspects of racial relations in Alabama include Peter Kolchin, *First Freedom: The Responses of Alabama's Blacks to Emancipation and Reconstruction* (Westport, Conn.: Greenwood Press, 1972); Horace Mann Bond, *Negro Education in Alabama: A Study in Cotton and Steel* (New York: Atheneum, 1939); William Warren Rogers and Robert David Ward, *August Reckoning: Jack Turner and Racism in Post-Civil War Alabama* (Baton Rouge: Louisiana State University Press, 1973); Louis R. Harlan, *Booker T. Washington: The Making of a Black Leader, 1856–1901* (New York: Harper and Row, 1971); and Dan T. Carter, *Scottsboro: A Tragedy of the American South* (Baton Rouge: Louisiana State University Press, 1969).

On the life of Alabama's white tenants, see the classic *Let Us Now Praise Famous Men* (New York: Ballantine Books, 1966), by James Agee and Walker Evans. For the life of a black tenant, see Theodore Rosengarten, *All God's Dangers: The Life of Nate Shaw* (New York: Alfred A. Knopf, 1975).

On Alabama's early coal, iron, and steel economy, see Ethel Armes, *The Story of Coal and Iron in Alabama* (1910; reprint, Birmingham: Book-keepers Press, 1972), and Robert David Ward and William Warren Rogers, *Labor Revolt in Alabama: The Great Strike of 1894* (University, Ala.: University of Alabama Press, 1965). For a study of the operations of an Alabama cotton plantation, see W. T.

Jordan, *Hugh Davis and His Alabama Plantation* (University, Ala.: University of Alabama Press, 1948).

An old work but still the only comprehensive treatment of its period is Walter L. Fleming, *Civil War and Reconstruction in Alabama* (Cleveland: Arthur H. Clark Co., 1911). An interesting collection of readings is Lucille Griffith, *Alabama: A Documentary History to 1900*, rev. ed., (University, Ala.: University of Alabama Press, 1972).

Social commentaries on Alabama during the 1930s include Carl Carmer, *Stars Fell on Alabama* (New York: Farrar and Rinehart, 1934), and Clarence Cason, *90° in the Shade* (Chapel Hill, N.C.: University of North Carolina Press, 1935).

It should be noted that this reading list does not pretend to be comprehensive. It has been prepared in answer to the editor's request for a brief list of additional books which may be of interest to lay people. Space limitations preclude the listing of numerous scholarly studies of the South and of this state.

Index

Abolitionism: among whites, 23–24, 116; and slavery issue, 24, 122; white hostility toward, 48, 111, 121, 145

Agriculture: and politics, 3, 37–42, 133, 145; practiced by Indians, 150. *See also* Crops

Alabama: admission to Union, 23; location of capital, 23; supreme court, 53, 89, 97, 142–143; Pardon and Parole Board, 90; archives, 124–125; capitol building, 125; Department of Pensions and Security, 126; prehistory, 149

—constitution: provision for manumission in, 24; reform of, 35; franchise provisions of, 40, 93–95; constitutional convention of 1867, 75

—legislature: representation in, 23, 35, 38–39, 133; and child labor law, 38; and establishment of public school system, 52; black members of, 72, 77, 101; and gerrymandering of congressional districts, 78; and Tuskegee Institute, 79, 80, 83; and question of annexation of Florida Panhandle, 161; mentioned, 24, 28, 74, 125, 145, 152

—sections: southeastern, 8, 9, 17, 28 (*see also* Wiregrass); coastal area, 160, 161–167 (*see also* Mobile); northern (*see* Hill country; Northern Alabama; Piedmont); south central (*see* Black Belt). *See also* map, facing 128

Alabama River: and fertile land of Black Belt, 10, 11; importance of to cotton trade, 120, 158; near Mobile, 151, 154; mentioned, 103, 111, 126

Architecture: of antebellum mansions, 106–113 *passim*

"A-Sleepin' at the Foot of the Bed," 36

Baptist Church: and frontier evangelism, 18, 19, 20, 21; mentioned, 7, 17

"Big Mules," 35, 37, 42

Birmingham: industrial development of, 12, 127–136; and anti-Catholic sentiment, 20; white leadership of, 35, 36, 137–146 *passim;* labor problems in, 39, 133–135; Klan activity in, 47; and civil rights issues, 97, 98, 100–101, 139–148; black leaders in, 100; settlement of, 128; founders of, 130; crime rate of, 135; in twentieth century, 136–148; muncipal finances and government of, 139, 141–142, 145–146; recent changes in, 147, 148; current economic situation of, 148; immigration to, 171; mentioned, 50, 51, 83, 93, 96

Black, Hugo Lafayette, 17, 33–34, 53, 141, 175–176

Black Belt: as symbol of romantic tradition, 5, 106–113; fertility of, 10, 12; concentration of slaves in, 23, 68; politics in, 40, 74, 77, 78, 91–94 *passim;* slave trade in, 56; settlement of, 103–105; women of, 113–119; at present, 125–127; and labor situation after Civil War, 133; Indians in, 150; and marketing of cotton, 158; mentioned, 11, 26, 84, 119, 120. *See also* Montgomery; Selma

Blacks: proposed colonization of, 23, 93, 174; and civil rights issues, 36, 41, 98–102, 141, 142; as voters, 40; and white violence, 44–48, 121; as viewed by poor whites, 45; conspiracies of feared by whites, 68, 86, 121; political leaders of during Reconstruction, 71–78; labor organization of, 73, 76; free, restrictions on, 75; as farmers, 76, 79, 82; education of, 78–84, 93; middle-class, 82, 93; disfranchisement of, 91–96, 124; in public office in twentieth century, 100, 101; as civic leaders, 100, 101–102; percentage of population in certain areas,

181

Republican party (*Cont.*)
outcasts, 174–175; mentioned, 42, 53, 124, 175. *See also* Radical Republicans
Rivers: importance of in mining coal, 13–14; as vital in development of Montgomery and Selma, 120, 123, 124; in cotton trade, 158; of Alabama and West Florida, 160
Roads: as political issue, 34, 35, 37
Roosevelt, Franklin D., 40, 90, 138, 176
Roosevelt, Theodore: and B. T. Washington, 81, 94–95; and purchase of TCI by U.S. Steel, 136; mentioned, 80, 93
Rural areas: catered to by politicians, 30–36; affected by federal programs, 41; visited by B. T. Washington, 79; of Dallas County, 123; life in, 126–127. *See also* Agriculture; Farmers

St. Clair County, 8, 22, 23, 27, 41, 44
"Savage Ideal," 5, 173, 176
Scandinavians, 128, 158, 162, 169, 170
Scotch-Irish: individualism and belligerence attributed to, 44, 51; and racism, 48; and Cajuns, 165; in Zidonia, 169; as white majority, 169; in conflict with Germans in Cullman, 171
Scottsboro trials, 47–48, 89–91, 98, 101, 176
Secession: controversy over, 24–26, 125; opposition to, 24–25, 28, 174; overwhelming support for in Montgomery County, 122–123; mentioned, 4, 31
Segregation: fought by James Rapier, 76–77; position of B. T. Washington on, 83; demonstrations against, 97–102; in Birmingham, 139–148; applied to Cajuns, 166. *See also* Civil rights; Desegregation
Selma: and Confederate armaments, 15, 120; slave trade in, 56, 123; and civil rights demonstrations, 97, 100, 101, 120, 124–125; black leaders in, 100; general history of, 123–125; and marketing of cotton, 123, 158; mentioned, 73, 77, 108, 125
Sharecropping, 37, 38, 80, 133
Sheffield, 50, 63, 133
Slaveholding: as related to Confederacy,

23, 28; distribution of in various parts of state, 23; high concentration of in Black Belt, 107, 120, 123; by Indians, 150; mentioned, 104. *See also* Slavery
Slavery: regarded as necessary for cotton culture in Black Belt, 11; and concept of slaves as legal property, 31; attitude of small farmers toward, 45; viewed by historians, 56–57, 63, 69, 70; viewed by former slaves, 58–71; religion of slaves, 68, 123; slave patrols, 68, 121, 123; viewed by planters' wives, 116; and southern guilt, 148; and French vineyard colony, 168; as alleged basis of South's defensive attitude, 173; debate over, 174; mentioned, 7, 10, 105, 111. *See also* Abolitionism; Blacks; Slaveholding
Sloss, James Withers, 127, 131, 132
Sloss-Sheffield Company, 12, 132, 133, 134
Social class: distinctions of valued, 51, 105, 163 (*see also* Social mobility); in Birmingham, 143; in antebellum Mobile, 156–157 (*see also* Gentry; Planters); middle—black, 82, 93; lower (*see* Poor whites)
Social equality, 81–82, 92
Social mobility, 22, 53, 105
Social services, 52, 138, 140; and single-tax system, 164. *See also* Federal government
Soto, Hernando de, 5, 151, 154
Spain: explorers from and Indians, 151, 154; control of Mobile by, 153, 154, 155; cession of Mobile area to U.S. by, 158; and effect on life in Mobile, 159–160; Spanish traders on Alabama rivers, 160; and West Florida, 160–161. *See also* Mobile
Steel industry, 130, 136, 139
Suffrage: universal, 77–78. *See also* Voting rights
Sumter County, 22, 70, 84
Supreme court (Ala.), 53, 89, 97, 142–143
Supreme Court (U.S.): *Brown* decision, 41, 176; Scottsboro Case, 89, 101; *Giles* v. *Harris*, 95–96; and Boswell amendment, 97; *Plessy* v. *Ferguson*, 99; and legislative reapportionment, 101; and steel pricing differential, 139; Hugo L. Black as

188

Index

Supreme Court (U.S.) (*Cont.*)
member of, 53, 176; mentioned, 96, 98, 99, 139

Tait, Charles, 104, 107, 126
Tax: poll, 35, 94, 95, 118; property, as political issue in Birmingham, 137, 138; avoided by U.S. Steel, 139
Tenantry, 37, 38, 80, 105, 133
Tennessee (Confederate ironclad), 15, 159
Tennessee Coal, Iron and Railroad Company, 132, 133, 134, 136, 143
Tennessee River, 9, 10, 149, 175; valley, 39, 106
Tombigbee River: and prime cotton land, 10, 103; and trade, 43, 158; mentioned, 151, 153, 161, 167
Tories (American Revolution), 154–155
"Tories" (Civil War), 25, 27, 29, 30, 174. *See also* Unionists
Transportation: at Huntsville, 10; of coal, 13–14; and issues of segregation, 76, 98–99, 101
Turner, Benjamin Sterling, 71, 72, 73–74, 78
Tuscaloosa: and civil rights demonstrations, 97, 99; replaced as capital by Montgomery, 122; mentioned, 12, 14, 24, 43, 108, 110, 125, 174
Tuskegee Institute, 79–83, 88, 96

Union army: enlistment of Alabama men in during Civil War, 26–27; Wilson's Raiders, 120, 124; mentioned, 7, 28, 69, 145, 162. *See also* Federal army
Unionists: in Alabama during Civil War, 24–30; former, terrorized by Klan, 46; in antebellum Montgomery and Selma, 122, 123; mentioned, 53, 95, 105
Unions: discouraged in cotton mills, 38; and coal industry, 39, 133–135; right to join, 41; benefits of to workers, 42; black, 73, 76; and conflict with nonunion labor, 133, 134; mentioned, 52, 145
United States Steel Corporation, 136, 139, 148
University of Alabama, 99, 108, 148
Urban areas: migration to, 35; benefited by redistricting, 41; and civil rights movement, 100

Vann, David, 141, 146, 147
Vigilance committees, 46, 89, 121. *See also* Ku Klux Klan; Lynching
Violence, 44–48, 51, 84–88, 121; and civil rights demonstrations, 141, 146; related to nonintellectualism, 144–145
Voting rights: curtailed, 40, 92–97, 98; and intervention by federal government, 41, 124, 125, 140; in civil rights demonstrations, 48, 101, 124–125; as seen by blacks, 81–82; in Reconstruction, 84, 85; exercised by blacks during Reconstruction, 91; in mid-twentieth century, 101; mentioned, 83. *See also* Civil rights

Wages: federal minimum, 40, 42, 140, 175; as labor issue, 134, 135; as factor in steel monopoly, 139; mentioned, 52
Wallace, George (gov.), 42, 53
War of 1812, 3, 22, 55, 162
Warrior River, 13, 14, 43, 44, 167
Washington, Booker T., 78–84, 93, 94
Wealth: in antebellum Montgomery and Selma, 122, 123; as motivation for industrial development, 127
Whig party, 122, 123
White population: general history of, 3–54, 103–119; antagonism of toward federal government, 41; violence of, 44–48, 121; and support of black aspirations after Civil War, 77; and support of B. T. Washington's ideas on black education, 80; and interest in Scottsboro trial, 90; of Montgomery and Selma, 121, 124; of Birmingham, in early twentieth century, 137; during desegregation crisis, 139–143. *See also* Planters; Poor whites; Slavery
White supremacy: maintained by manipulation of black votes, 40, 91–97, 124; as alleged motive of Klansmen, 46; and Democratic party, 91, 96; and violence, 121; and segregation in Birmingham, 140. *See also* Racism, Violence
Whitfield, Gen. Nathan Bryan, 108, 109, 110
Wilcox County, 22, 82, 104, 125; black population of, 94, 124
Winston County: relatively few slaves in,